The Teacher's Choice

Ideas and Activities for Teaching Basic Skills

Sandra Nina Kaplan

Sheila Kunishima Madsen

Bette Taylor Gould

Goodyear Publishing Company, Inc.

Santa Monica, California

31928

Library of Congress Cataloging in Publication Data

Kaplan, Sandra Nina.
    The teacher's choice.

    (Goodyear series in education)
    Includes index.
    1. Education, Elementary—Curricula.   2. Elementary
school teaching.   I. Madsen, Sheila K., 1940–   joint
author.   II. Gould, Bette Taylor, 1943–   joint author.
III. Title.
LB1570.K283   372.1′1′02   77-17223
ISBN 0-87620-900-2
ISBN 0-87620-899-5 pbk.

Y-8995-6 (paper)
Y-9002-0 (case)

Current Printing (last digit)
10 9 8 7 6 5 4 3 2 1

Printed in the United States of America

Cover design: Matt Pomaski

Interior design: Roger Trietley

Illustrations: Anna Pomaska

Project editor: Georgia Griggs

CONTENTS

31928

WORKSHEET CONTENTS

Note: Titles in bold-face type are
Assessment or Record-Keeping worksheets.

INTRODUCTION

Teachers continually make choices that affect themselves as teachers and children as learners. Although the school and community expect teachers to make choices that accommodate to the particular needs, abilities, and interests of each student, often too little attention is paid to the needs, abilities, and interests of the teachers.

We feel that choices regarding the learning needs of students cannot be made without a corresponding reference to the instructional needs of teachers. In recognizing the teacher's, as well as the student's, right to individuality, we have developed a variety of activities for teaching basic skills within several instructional modes. This book is based on the assumption that teachers know what and how to teach. It is responsive to their need for activities that enhance instructional choices already made, and suggests other modes they can try. *The Teacher's Choice* provides alternatives for matching what students need for learning basic skills to what teachers need for effective teaching.

Current discussions about the basics often try to resolve issues such as which basics are most important, what degree of emphasis should be placed on basic skills, and what methods are best for teaching the basics. One usual point of agreement is that learning the basics is a vital aspect of schooling.

A point of disagreement is that drill is the best way to teach and master basic skills. We believe the presentation of the basics in a variety of instructional modes and activities provides for more effective transfer of learning and reinforcement. One way to reinforce basic skills so that they are meaningful and interesting to learners is to integrate them with content from many subject areas and everyday materials; activities using everyday materials—labeled Relevant Reinforcers—are included in Part 2.

Our definition of the basics, while including traditional categories of reading, writing, and arithmetic skills, is extended into other areas. For example, concepts and skills that are fundamental to understanding any subject can be defined as basics. Some basic skills, such as making inferences, are general to many areas while others, such as knowing the symbols for chemical elements, are specific to a given subject area. We have selected basic skills from each of the above categories, although we realize there are many other basic skills for which activities could be developed.

BASIC SKILL SETS

Each basic skill set of activities in Part 1 is divided into the following sections:

Assessment Worksheets

These worksheets focus on assessing several skills within a broader skill topic. Each one is a model illustrating a different type of testing format, and thus provides children with a variety of test-taking practice. Generally, two kinds of assessment worksheets are provided. Some are for children to complete independently, while others are to be completed, at least in part, with the teacher or other monitor.

Record-Keeping Worksheets

These pages provide skill and subskill headings and grids for recording the successes and problems of groups of students. Some

suggest or provide a simple assessment procedure to be used in obtaining skill information.

General Activities

This section contains a set of five or six activities that focus on the subskills related to the major skill heading. As a group, these activities provide for a variety of learning modalities and range from easy to difficult. Each activity may be used in any instructional mode, including the ones discussed below.

Learning Center

The learning center overview illustrates ways to display the skill activities and materials with the intent of providing opportunities for student self-selection and decision making. Each learning center includes a variety of materials to accommodate various learning modalities and abilities and depicts a different way to organize center activities.

Group Work

These activities may be used with either teacher-directed or independent groups. They are designed to teach skills while encouraging interaction with others, promoting cooperative learning, and developing self-concept.

Independent Study

Some activities in this section require the use of a basic skill while studying a self-selected topic. Other activities extend the use of a skill by providing more difficult or unusual practice experiences.

Integrating with the Real World

These activities provide for the application of skills in real-life situations. They fulfill a need for relevant, meaningful application of skills by using everyday materials with which children are familiar. Home/community involvement is emphasized in many of the activities.

Although all the activities, except those in General Activities, are included within particular instructional modes, they can be adapted or modified for other uses. Following are some of the alternative uses:

- Student self-selected activity after completion of assignments.
- Instructional assistance for teacher, tutor, or aide.
- Parent/student at-home learning experiences.
- Review of a skill previously mastered.
- Independent learning aid.
- Followup to a teacher-directed lesson.
- Teaching aid that motivates or introduces a skill lesson.
- Learning-center task.
- Learning-station task.
- Diagnostic tool to assess or evaluate student needs, interests, and learnings.
- Assessment tool to aid in forming teaching groups.
- Independent study stimulant.
- Single activities or as part of a collection for a unit of study.
- Reinforcement or remedial practice.
- Record-keeping or reporting instrument.
- Diagnostic/prescriptive tool.
- Pre/post-evaluative test.

RELEVANT REINFORCERS

The activities in Part 2 capitalize on the children's interest in and familiarity with real-world materials by redirecting the purpose for which these materials are generally used so that they become educational tools. The term relevant, in this context, refers to activities that are related to the child's real world through the use of everyday products and materials. The term reinforcers means that these activities provide additional practice for skills that have been previously taught. For the teacher, relevant reinforcers are:

- Easy-to-make activities from readily obtainable materials.
- High-interest-level learning activities constructed from relatively inexpensive or free materials.
- Materials to use in assessing students' ability to transfer learned skills to different situations.

How to Make Your Own Relevant Reinforcers

1. Make a collection of things that are readily available in multiples, such as:

postcards	catalogs
price tags, sales slips	toys
junk mail	food
product coupons	clothing
empty packages	maps

2. Select one set and list the properties and contents of each item in it. Example:

Item	*Contents*	*Properties*
maps	cities	900 square inches
	rivers	8 folds of the map
	mileage	

3. Identify the skills children need to practice and correlate them with appropriate properties or contents. Examples:

Skills	*Properties/Contents*
alphabetizing	cities
measuring	rivers
syllables	mileage

4. List tasks children can do to illustrate what they have learned. Examples:

   divide
   list
   match
   connect
   illustrate

5. Match a task children perform to show their learnings with a basic skill and the properties or contents of the item. Example:

   List ten cities from the map; divide them into syllables.

6. Write the tasks on the items. Provide additional items for children to work on.

1

BASIC SKILL SETS

ASSESSMENT WORKSHEET

FOLLOWING DIRECTIONS

1. Write your name in the upper right-hand corner. Circle the first and last letter. Write the date under your name.
2. Write your name on the line in the lower left-hand corner.
3. Write your first initial and your last name above the box in the upper left-hand corner.
4. Write your initials in the circle. Underline your last initial.
5. Write your name in capital letters in the boxes in the lower right-hand corner. Use one box for each letter. Color in any empty boxes.
6. Write your last name down the left-hand side and your first name down the right-hand side of the paper. Number each letter in your name.
7. Write your last name to the right of the X. Cross out every other letter.

Teacher option: Have student follow oral directions to
               complete a task _____
               go to a location _____

X

First name
Middle name
Last name

Last name first

Reproducible, page 133.
Solution, page 191.

SKILLS IN THIS SECTION INCLUDE:

- following written and oral directions
- reading and writing directions
- developing vocabulary related to following directions

Following Directions

GENERAL ACTIVITIES

RIDDLE PUZZLE WORKSHEET

skill: following written directions

RIDDLE PUZZLE   Name_____

Directions:
1. Count 5 rows down. Write the four-letter word starting in the 4th square.
2. Count 5 columns across. Reading down, write the word starting in the 5th square from the top.
3. Find the 10th column across. Write the word starting in the last 4 squares of this column.
4. Write the word made with every other letter in the second row down.
5. Count down to the 5th, 6th, and 7th rows. Write the word made from the 1st letter in each row.
6. Count across to the 9th column. Write the five-letter word that begins with the 1st letter in this column.

Do you know the answer to the riddle? If not, follow these directions.

1. Write the 1st letter in the 2nd row from the bottom.
2. Write the seven-letter word that is in the 4th row down, beginning in the 3rd square.
3. Find the 7th column across. Write the word that begins with the 5th letter in this column.

T	H	I	N	T	S	Q	U	F	E	L
W	O	H	O	E	H	E	T	L	M	S
O	P	E	N	R	G	B	D	I	X	E
Z	E	G	A	R	B	A	G	E	T	R
A	C	O	W	H	A	T	E	S	O	I
N	E	B	S	A	R	R	T	U	V	P
D	L	E	K	S	O	U	P	M	F	E
E	T	R	I	P	L	C	L	A	O	K
A	S	Q	W	A	L	K	O	R	U	N
L	A	W	G	M	A	N	T	K	R	O

Write the words you find here: _____

_____

For fun:
There are at least 21 words hidden in the rows and 21 words hidden in the columns, besides the words you just wrote. Can you find them?

Reproducible, page 134.
Solution, page 191.

TOUR ITINERARIES

*skills: following written directions to a location
writing directions*

Children can also practice writing directions themselves by preparing tours for other students to follow.

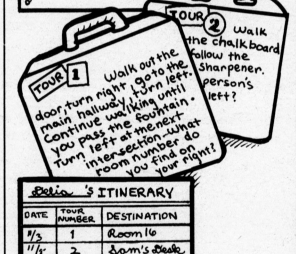

"TAKE A TOUR"
1. Choose any tour.
2. Follow the directions.
3. Record your tour number and destination on your itinerary.

TOUR 1 Walk out the door, turn right. go to the main hallway, turn left. Continue walking until you pass the fountain. Turn left at the next intersection—What room number do you find on your right?

TOUR 2 Walk the chalkboard follow the sharpener. person's left?

Delia 's ITINERARY

DATE	TOUR NUMBER	DESTINATION
11/3	1	Room 16
11/5	2	Sam's Desk

MAP FILL-IN WORKSHEET

*skills: following written directions of geographical terms
following directions to create a map and a legend*

Variation:

Cut out a variety of shapes for children to use in making maps. Children then choose a shape, outline it, and fill it in, following either the directions on this worksheet or directions written by someone else.

MAP FILL-IN   Name _____

1. Read all the directions below before starting to fill in the map.
2. Use color and symbols to show:
   a river running from north to south
   two roads crossing the river
   two bridges for the roads
   a large swamp area between the two roads, east of the river
   an airport in the southeast
   a town on the western bank of the river, south of the southernmost road
   a church northwest of the northernmost road
   a mountain range west of the river
   a school west of the town
   two streams running from the mountain range into the river
3. Complete the legend to show what the colors and symbols on your map stand for.

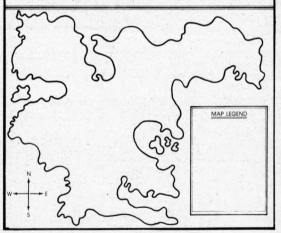

MAP LEGEND

N W E S

Reproducible, page 135.
Solution, page 192.

GENERAL ACTIVITIES

BEANBAG TOSS ART

skill: understanding prepositions used in directions

Children toss beanbags until they have landed one in each column of the chart. They then draw a picture to correspond to the words indicated by the beanbags.

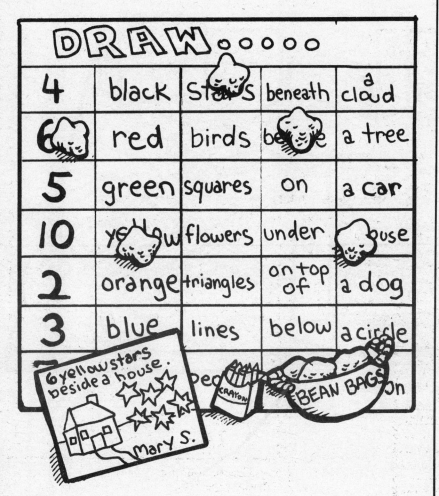

DRAW ○○○○○			
4	black	stars	beneath	a cloud
6	red	birds	beside	a tree
5	green	squares	on	a car
10	yellow	flowers	under	a house
2	orange	triangles	on top of	a dog
3	blue	lines	below	a circle

6 yellow stars beside a house.

Mary S.

MAKE-A-GAME SQUARES

skill: following written directions that use gameboard vocabulary

Using themselves as markers, children move the number of steps indicated on the die and follow the directions on the square they land on. Rules regarding what happens if more than one child lands on the same square need to be formalized with the class—*before* starting.

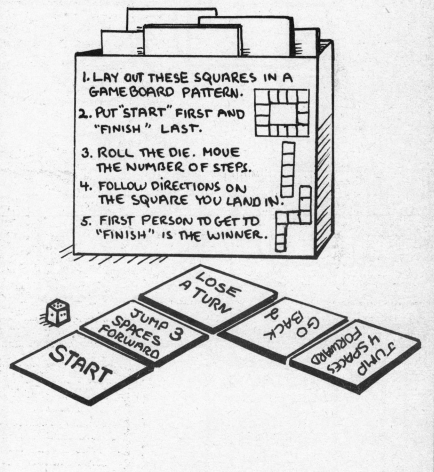

1. LAY OUT THESE SQUARES IN A GAMEBOARD PATTERN.
2. PUT "START" FIRST AND "FINISH" LAST.
3. ROLL THE DIE. MOVE THE NUMBER OF STEPS.
4. FOLLOW DIRECTIONS ON THE SQUARE YOU LAND IN.
5. FIRST PERSON TO GET TO "FINISH" IS THE WINNER.

LOSE A TURN

JUMP 3 SPACES FORWARD

GO BACK 4

JUMP 4 SPACES FORWARD

START

LEARNING CENTER

Materials are displayed in a gameboard format. Children may move through the materials sequentially or be assigned activities related to their needs.

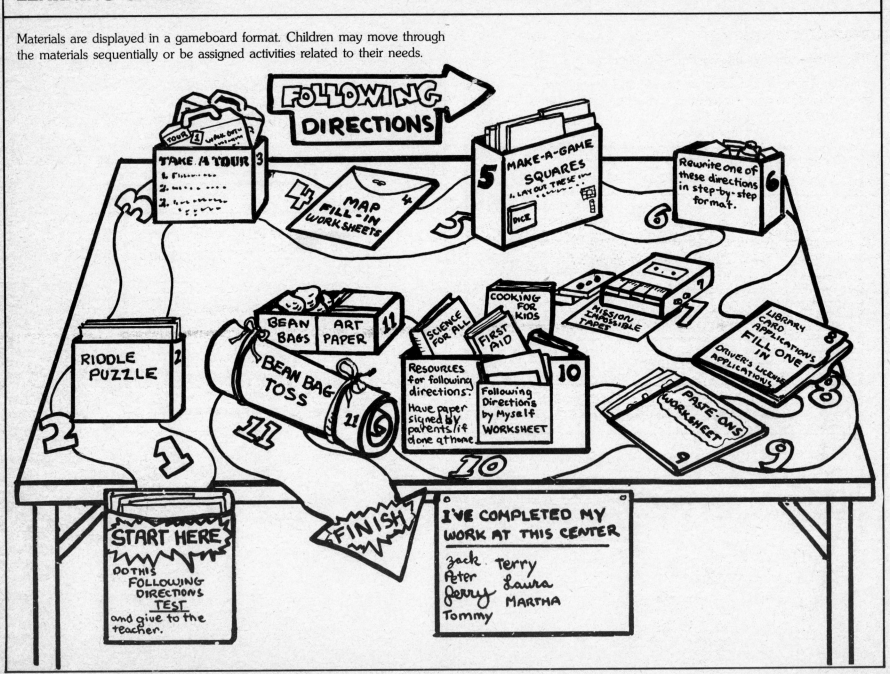

GROUP WORK

MARK IT

skill: understanding verbs and prepositions used in directions

Provide children with a picture or word worksheet made from coloring-book pages or word lists. Incorporate words from your chart in oral or written directions for students to mark their worksheets in various ways. If the objective of the activity is to practice following oral directions, do not show the chart until children's work is to be corrected. If the objective is to practice reading the direction words, point to a word on the chart and tell children to mark an object on their worksheets in the way indicated.

INDEPENDENT STUDY

FOLLOWING DIRECTIONS BY MYSELF WORKSHEET

skill: following written and oral directions

Display worksheet with a variety of resources such as science books, recipe books or files, forms, and first-aid manuals.

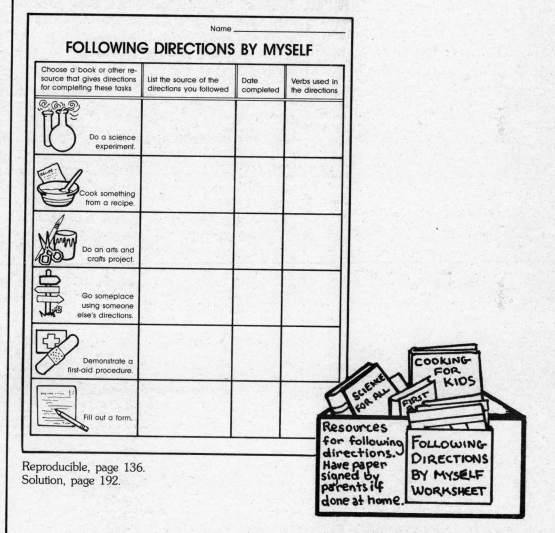

Reproducible, page 136.
Solution, page 192.

INDEPENDENT STUDY

INTEGRATING WITH THE REAL WORLD

MISSION IMPOSSIBLE CASSETTES

skill: following oral directions

Make a set of "Mission Impossible" cassettes. Each cassette contains directions for accomplishing a task. A child chooses a cassette, listens to the directions for one task, and tries to complete the task from memory. Students check their work by replaying the cassettes. Cassettes may be color- or number-coded for levels of difficulty, depending on the number of steps given in the directions.

Variation:
Taped directions may direct children to certain books, library shelves, or study prints from which they choose an independent study topic.

REWRITING DIRECTIONS

skill: rewriting directions in step-by-step form

Find instructions that are written in paragraph form, such as directions on cleaning products, cosmetics, and appliances. Children rewrite the directions in brief, numbered, step-by-step format using key words and main ideas.

FILLING IN FORMS

skill: filling in real applications and forms

Collect a variety of forms in multiples for children to practice filling out. Some forms available in most areas are library card applications, bicycle registrations, catalog order blanks, and driver's license applications.

PASTE-ONS WORKSHEET

*skills: following written directions
understanding common verbs and prepositions used in directions*

Reproducible, page 137.

ASSESSMENT WORKSHEET

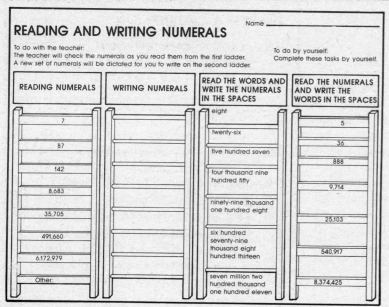

READING AND WRITING NUMERALS

Name _____

To do with the teacher:
The teacher will check the numerals as you read them from the first ladder.
A new set of numerals will be dictated for you to write on the second ladder.

To do by yourself:
Complete these tasks by yourself.

READING NUMERALS	WRITING NUMERALS	READ THE WORDS AND WRITE THE NUMERALS IN THE SPACES	READ THE NUMERALS AND WRITE THE WORDS IN THE SPACES
7		eight	5
87		twenty-six	36
142		five hundred seven	888
8,683		four thousand nine hundred fifty	9,714
35,705		ninety-nine thousand one hundred eight	25,103
491,660		six hundred seventy-nine thousand eight hundred thirteen	540,917
6,172,979		seven million two hundred thousand one hundred eleven	8,374,425
Other:			

Reproducible, page 138.
Solution, page 192.

SKILLS IN THIS SECTION INCLUDE:

- translating number words into numerals and numerals into number words
- counting
- analyzing number patterns

Reading and Writing Numerals

GENERAL ACTIVITIES

CAPTURE THE NUMBERS

skills: *writing numerals from number words*
writing numerals in order

Write number words on a spinner, and make a corresponding recording sheet. The numbers may vary depending on the children's needs.

Variation:
Make spinners with other sets of numbers such as even or odd.

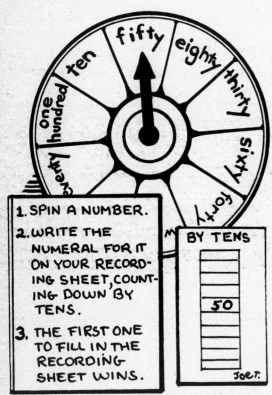

1. SPIN A NUMBER.
2. WRITE THE NUMERAL FOR IT ON YOUR RECORDING SHEET, COUNTING DOWN BY TENS.
3. THE FIRST ONE TO FILL IN THE RECORDING SHEET WINS.

BY TENS

50

JOE T.

1-2-3

skills: *counting*
counting by even and odd numbers

Number index cards or the backs of old playing cards with numerals from 1 to 50. Deal out all the cards to three or four players, including one extra hand that is set aside and not used in the game. The lowest card in the first player's hand is discarded face up. Any player, including the first one, who has the next number in sequence lays it down, and so on. Each player must call out the number discarded. Whenever no one has the next card in sequence, the last player to have played a card starts a new sequence with the lowest card left in his or her hand. The first player to play all cards is the winner.

Variation:
Sets of cards may also be made with other numbering patterns, such as even and odd numbers, or numerals from 50 to 100.

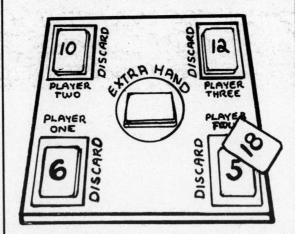

THREE'S A CROWD

skills: *matching sets to numerals*
counting

Variation:
Write number words instead of numerals in the gameboard spaces.

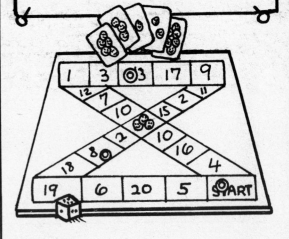

DIRECTIONS: 2 to 4 PLAYERS
1. Deal five cards to each player.
2. Roll the die to move.
3. If a card in your hand matches the numeral on the space you land in, discard it. If you don't have a match, the next player goes. Any player who lands on the "three's a crowd" space may move to any other space.
4. The first player to discard all cards is the winner.

GENERAL ACTIVITIES

SIZABLE SUMS WORKSHEET

skills: writing large numbers from number words

writing number words from numerals

SIZABLE SUMS	Name_____
Write the sums in number words	Show your work here in numerals
1. ten thousand four hundred plus eighty-five equals	
2. six hundred fifty-seven plus one hundred thirty-two equals	
3. nine hundred twenty-three million two hundred seventy-one thousand sixty-six plus ten million five thousand eight hundred ten equals	
4. four hundred billion twelve million three thousand six hundred thirty-two plus one billion ten million one thousand two hundred two equals	
5. nine hundred forty billion thirty-six million seven hundred twenty-five thousand four plus one million two hundred three thousand nine hundred thirteen equals	

Reproducible, page 139.
Solution, page 192.

NUMBER POEM WORKSHEET

skill: writing numerals from number words

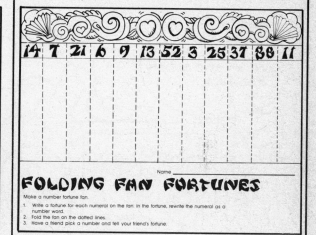

Name_____

NUMBER POEM

I once met a man on his way to St. Ives,
He had two thousand four hundred ninety-two wives.

One thousand two cats,
Six hundred three hats,
And two hundred thirty-six one-eyed bats.

He carried a pail of two thousand ten frogs,
And was chased by one hundred twenty-three dogs.
His seventeen sons wore eighty-five shirts,
And his daughter wore five hundred forty-eight skirts.

They all did arrive,
In the town of St. Ives,
And forever after lived wonderful lives.

Write the numerals to tell how many of the things below are in the poem:

_____ wives   _____ hats   _____ frogs
_____ cats   _____ bats   _____ dogs
_____ sons   _____ shirts   _____ skirts
_____ daughters

List and find the total number of:
PEOPLE   ANIMALS   CLOTHES

Reproducible, page 140.
Solution, page 193.

FOLDING FAN FORTUNES WORKSHEET

skill: writing number words from numerals

14 7 21 6 9 13 52 3 25 37 88 11

Name_____

FOLDING FAN FORTUNES

Make a number fortune fan.

1. Write a fortune for each numeral on the fan. In the fortune, rewrite the numeral as a number word.
2. Fold the fan on the dotted lines.
3. Have a friend pick a number and tell your friend's fortune.

Reproducible, page 141.
Solution, page 193.

LEARNING CENTER

Attaching bags, manila envelopes, and boxes to a wall or bulletin board is a space-saving way to display center materials. Children can take an activity to another area to work on, leaving their "number names" or other markers in the space from which the activity was removed. This will let others know where the activity is, and can be used by the teacher to keep track of the activities each child has worked on.

GROUP WORK

BIG NUMBER CHARTS

skill: reading large numbers

Make a set of charts, each with two rows of nine spaces. Cover each chart with clear contact paper. Construct a spinner that shows several digits in each section. Each child takes a chart and writes with a grease pencil or crayon the numerals from 1 to 9 in any order across the top row. Turn the spinner. Students write the numerals shown on the spinner directly beneath the corresponding numerals already on the chart, and fill in any empty spaces with zeroes. Children take turns reading aloud the number shown on the bottom row of their charts.

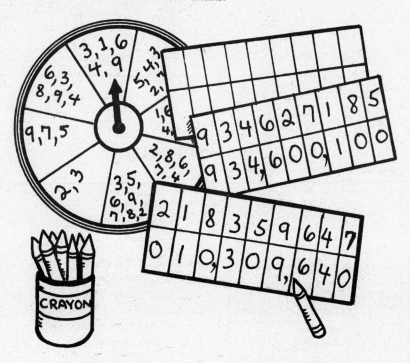

INDEPENDENT STUDY

BACK TO BASES

skills: researching number systems
converting numbers to other systems

Give children practice in reading and writing numbers in other bases and in different number systems, such as Roman or Egyptian, by adapting the numbers or directions for any activity in the basic collection.

A 5, eight, eleven, 14, 17, twenty, twenty-three, 26...
Continue the pattern with 6 more examples.

B 5, ten, 7, twelve, 9, fourteen...
Continue the pattern with 6 more examples.

C 8, eighteen, 108, one thousand eight, 10,008, one hundred thousand eight, 1,000,008, 6...
Continue the pattern with 6 more examples.

D 30, thirty, twenty-seven, 37, thirty-seven, thirty-four, 44...
Continue the pattern to sixty-five.

NUMBER PATTERNS

skills: continuing number patterns
reading and writing numeral
and number sequences

Make children aware of the numeral/word pattern as well as the computational pattern on their strips.

NUMBER PATTERN ANSWER KEY

A. 29, thirty-two, thirty-five, 38, 41, fourty-four.

B. 11, sixteen, 13, eighteen, 15, twenty.

C. sixteen, 106, one thousand six, 10,006, one hundred thousand six, 1,000,006.

D. forty-four, forty-one, 51, fifty-one, forty-seven, 57, fifty-seven, fifty-three, 63, sixty three, fifty-nine, 69, sixty-nine, 65.

INTEGRATING WITH THE REAL WORLD

NUMBER MURAL

skill: seeing practical applications of numerals

Draw several starter objects that display numbers on a large piece of paper. Store a variety of art materials nearby. Children add to the mural any real-world objects that display numbers in some way. The objects may be drawn or cut from magazines.

REAL-WORLD NUMBER CHARTS

skill: identifying commonly used numerals

Write commonly used numbers at the tops of several charts. Children add examples to these charts of how or where the numbers are used in the real world.

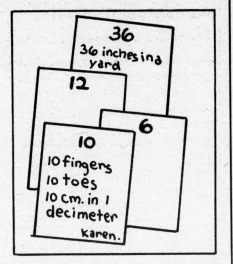

COLLECTIONS

skills: counting
writing numerals
estimating
making collections

Children choose everyday objects to collect. They date and label their collections to show the number of objects in them. Whenever additions are made to the collections, the children should make new labels to show the current number of objects in the collections.

RECORD-KEEPING WORKSHEET

BASIC NUMBER FACTS

Use the code to record students' readiness, practice, and mastery of basic facts related to the various math processes.

CODE

⊠ indicates readiness

⊠ indicates student is studying or practicing; enter date when mastery is achieved

STUDENTS' NAMES	SKILLS											
	+			−			×			÷		
	BASIC FACTS (through 18)	SOLVING WORD PROBLEMS	APPLYING FACTS TO NEW SITUATIONS	BASIC FACTS (through 18)	SOLVING WORD PROBLEMS	APPLYING FACTS TO NEW SITUATIONS	BASIC FACTS (through 10's)	SOLVING WORD PROBLEMS	APPLYING FACTS TO NEW SITUATIONS	BASIC FACTS (dividends to 100)	SOLVING WORD PROBLEMS	APPLYING FACTS TO NEW SITUATIONS

Reproducible, page 142.

SKILLS IN THIS SECTION INCLUDE:

- practicing addition, subtraction, multiplication, and division facts
- writing and solving word problems
- understanding the concept of number and basic facts
- using many number names for the same number

Basic Number Facts

GENERAL ACTIVITIES

LET'S MAKE A DEAL

skill: practicing recall of math facts

Provide sixty flashcards of the processes being studied (addition, subtraction, multiplication, or division). Place five flashcards in each "door."

JEOPARDY WORKSHEET

*skills: developing word problems to fit a given
        sum, remainder, product, or quotient
        writing equations for word problems*

Variation:
Make the worksheet into a large gameboard, using different topics and playing teams.

JEOPARDY   Name —————

To use as a worksheet for one person:

For each topic, write a related word problem and number equation in the boxes. The answers will be the numbers in the boxes.

To use as a game: (4 players)

1. Three of the players are contestants and the fourth is the moderator.
2. Each contestant selects a topic and writes word problems and equations for each numeral in his or her column. When a contestant completes a column, the moderator verifies the problems.
3. Contestants who correctly use all the numerals in their columns win.

🍔 FOOD 🍔	🐛 ANIMALS 🐛	🚗 CARS 🚗
6	4	2
8	9	10
10	14	16
81	24	36

Reproducible, page 143.
Solution, page 193.

NAME THAT FACT

*skill: developing many basic fact names for the
        same number*

Make up a set of number cards. A moderator holds up a card. Two contestants make bids for how many different number names they think they will be able to write for that number. The bids continue to get higher until one contestant says, "Name that fact." The other contestant must then write the same amount of different number names as his or her last bid. If successful, the contestant earns the same number of points as the bid.

GENERAL ACTIVITIES

HOLLYWOOD SQUARES

skill: practicing recall of math facts

Draw a tic-tac-toe grid on the chalkboard or on a laminated chart. In this game there are nine stars, two contestants, and a moderator. Contestants, in turn, play tic-tac-toe by choosing a star to respond to a number fact selected randomly from flashcards and presented by the moderator. If the star is correct the contestant takes possession of the star's square with X or O. The first contestant to get tic-tac-toe wins.

WHEEL OF FORTUNE

skill: practicing recall of math facts

Make a large Wheel of Fortune spinner to be used with a collection of flashcards. The object of the game is for players to fill their Pots o' Gold with the most cards.

DIRECTIONS: 2-4 PLAYERS

1. Spin the wheel to find out how many flashcards to answer.

2. Put each card answered correctly into your Pot o' Gold.

3. If you answer all correctly, spin again.

4. When you do not answer correctly, it is the next player's turn.

THE PYRAMID GAME WORKSHEET

skill: practicing recall of math facts within a given time limit

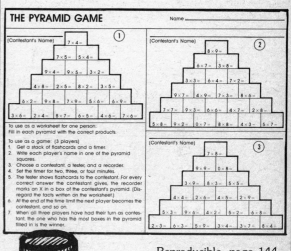

Reproducible, page 144.
Solution, page 193.

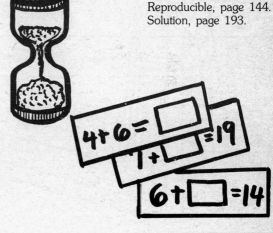

LEARNING CENTER

Chart racks may be moved outside the room or to some other area so that children who are working quietly will not be disturbed. Chart racks at this center may be placed inside a television box to make the game-show idea more real and appealing. Sign-up lists are a way for the children to indicate the games they have played.

GROUP WORK

STORY LINE

skills: writing number equations to illustrate number line activities using the number line

Paste picture labels or draw pictures for each numeral on a number line. Children write number equations to match stories told by a classmate or the teacher. For example, "The butterfly flew to the rose and then flew on to the house" is translated into the equation $2 + 3 = 5$. The direction of the action described in the story indicates the operation children are to use to write the equation.

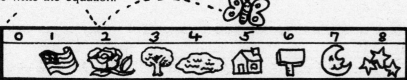

CHAIN GANG

skill: using real objects to demonstrate basic number facts

Provide each child with an ample supply of paper clips. Read math statements to the children and have them make paper-clip chains for each step. The chains can be linked to show addition or multiplication or broken to show subtraction or division. Once children understand the manipulation of real objects, number facts may be presented in representational drawings and then in standard symbolic form.

Put together 2 Clips.
Now clip 3 together.
Put both chains together.
How many do you have?

2
+3
5

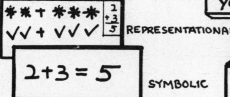

REPRESENTATIONAL

$2 + 3 = 5$

SYMBOLIC

PAPER CLIPS

INDEPENDENT STUDY

NUMBER BOXES

skill: demonstrating understanding of numbers and basic number facts

Place collections of real objects or paper markers in separate boxes labeled with numerals. Write tasks that are appropriate to the math concepts being studied. Children can be assigned a particular task or they can select a task that matches their needs or interests.

1. Make up a fact that equals this number or a division fact that uses this number as a dividend.
2. Use objects or markers to show the fact.
3. Draw pictures to show the fact.
4. Use symbols to write the fact.
5. Make up a problem or situation to match the fact.

1.
3.
Monty
$6 \div 3 = 2$

INDEPENDENT STUDY

TABLE-OF-CONTENTS MATH

skills: recognizing number names
understanding place value

Collect a variety of math materials, including textbooks, kits, and worksheet files. Develop a Table of Contents chart to go with the materials. Assign children, individually or in groups, to the parts appropriate to their needs or interests. Children use the number names to find out how many problems to do and where the problems can be found.

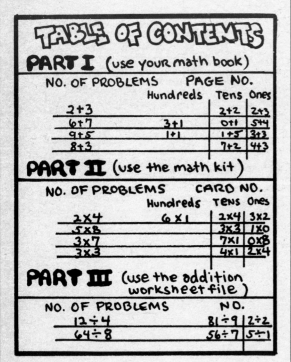

INTEGRATING WITH THE REAL WORLD

IT'S THE REAL THING WORKSHEET

skills: developing many number names for the same number
writing equations

Name _____

IT'S THE REAL THING

1. Get a real six-pack container, muffin tin, pair of gloves, and egg carton.
2. Write math signs ($+$, $-$, $\times$, $\div$) on the drawings below to show the kinds of basic facts you will make.
3. Group real objects (buttons, beans, bottle tops) in the containers to show all the ways you can make that number.
4. Write equations for each number name you discover on the lines beside the drawings.

Reproducible, page 145.
Solution, page 194.

ASSESSMENT WORKSHEET

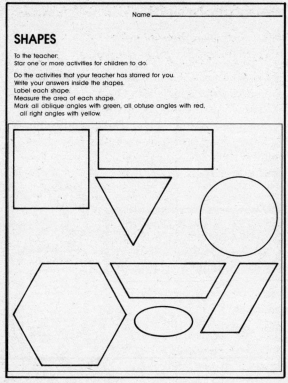

Name _____

SHAPES

To the teacher:
Star one or more activities for children to do.

Do the activities that your teacher has starred for you.
Write your answers inside the shapes.
Label each shape.
Measure the area of each shape.
Mark all oblique angles with green, all obtuse angles with red,
  all right angles with yellow.

Reproducible, page 146.
Solution, page 194.

SKILLS IN THIS SECTION INCLUDE:

- identifying, constructing, measuring, and using geometric shapes
- developing vocabulary related to geometry
- applying geometry skills and knowledge in different contexts

Geometry

GENERAL ACTIVITIES

PLAY THE ANGLES

skills: naming angles
computing area
measuring line segments

Make up a Play the Angles worksheet and set of cards. Duplicate the worksheet and distribute to each player. Children take turns selecting cards and drawing angles on their worksheets. There may be several kinds of winners: the player who has the most enclosed shapes, the greatest amount of total area within all enclosed shapes, or the longest total length of line segments.

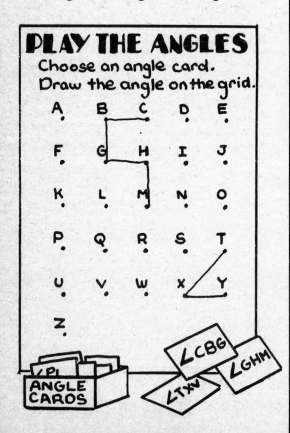

GEOMETRIC EQUATIONS

skills: identifying and constructing shapes

Children choose a card and translate the equation by drawing or cutting and pasting to show what steps they went through.

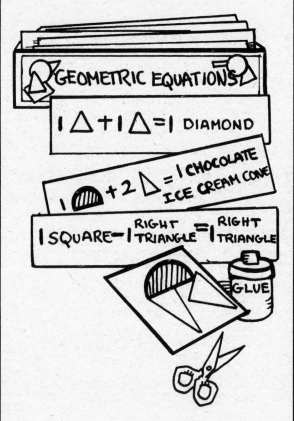

GEOMETER GEORGE

skills: vocabulary development
using vocabulary in context

Select from textbooks the geometric vocabulary appropriate for your class. List the verbs and process words used in geometry in one column of a large chart and the words naming geometric forms, shapes, or objects in the second column. Children choose problems to solve from Geometer George.

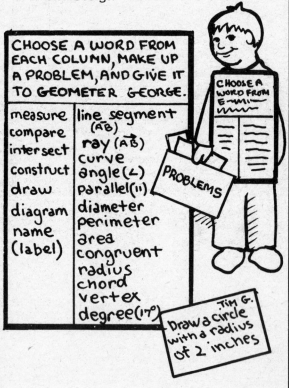

GENERAL ACTIVITIES

GEO DESIGNS

skills: computing areas
adding and subtracting areas

Make shapes of differing dimensions and label as floor plans. Also make up a simple recording sheet with additional questions, such as: What is the total area of all the floor plans you measured? What is the difference in size between the largest and smallest floor plans?

360° GAME

skill: Using a protractor to measure and draw angles

Each player begins with a straight line that has a point in the middle. Players take turns choosing angle cards and using a protractor to construct and label angles on their line. Each angle must be tangent to the preceding one. The first player to draw 360° around the line is the winner.

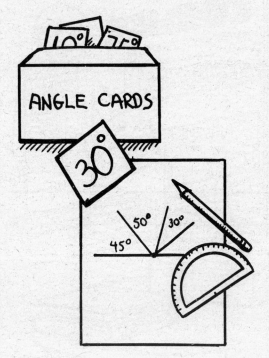

COLOR THE SHAPES WORKSHEET

skill: identifying geometric shapes

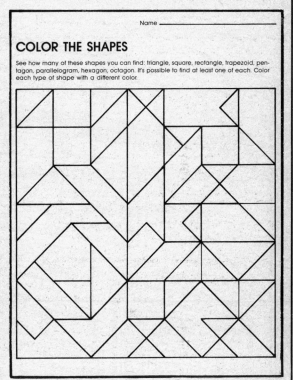

Reproducible, page 147.
Solution, page 194.

LEARNING CENTER

A folding screen can be used to partition off a center from the rest of the room and provide a space in which children can work. Direction cards posted at the center direct the students to make use of its equipment and furniture in skill tasks.

GROUP WORK

GAMEBOARD DESIGNS

skills: developing geometric products
problem solving

Discuss the layout and count the squares on a checkerboard. Provide materials for children to use in designing and making new checkerboards, incorporating geometric shapes other than squares. As students use the new boards to play checkers, discuss the rules and rewrite them to adapt the game to the new board designs. This process can be repeated for other familiar gameboards such as Parcheesi, Monopoly, and tic-tac-toe.

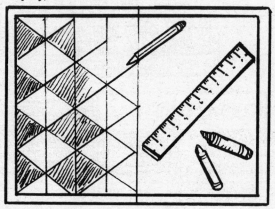

WORD-CARD GAMES

skill: understanding and identifying geometric
terms and forms

With the group's help, list words naming geometric processes and figures, and have children make cards of these words. Write directions for several simple games such as Go Fish, Lotto, and Concentration. Children use the word cards to play the games. Games may be stored for later independent use.

INDEPENDENT STUDY

GEOMETRIC ART GALLERY

skills: reproducing geometric shapes
problem solving

Children reproduce a picture from the gallery by identifying, measuring, and drawing shapes and then coloring their reproductions.

Variations:
Children can use the same shapes and dimensions found in the picture but rearrange them into a different pattern. Or they can use the same shapes and patterns but alter the dimensions of the shapes.

PROVE IT ENVELOPES

skills: demonstrating proofs for geometric statements
problem solving

Fill each PROVE IT envelope with objects needed to illustrate a proof. Children choose envelopes, prove the statements or formulas, and record the process and outcomes on a teacher-made worksheet or blank sheet of paper.

INDEPENDENT STUDY

RESEARCHING GEOMETERS

skills: research
writing true/false statements

List the names of famous geometers such as Euclid, Pythagoras, Anaxagoras, and Plato. Children choose one to research and write a series of true/false statements about the geometer to try out on their friends.

INTEGRATING WITH THE REAL WORLD

GEOMETRIC GREETING CARDS

skills: drawing geometric shapes
making collages

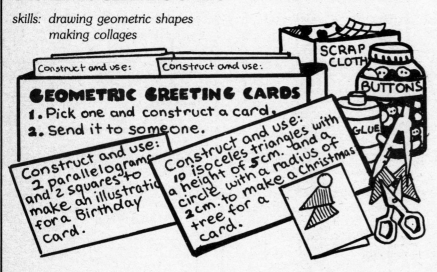

GEOMETRIC EXHIBITS

skill: seeing shapes in everyday objects

Children set up geometric exhibits based on themes such as foods, toys, and fantasy. Objects on display are to be labeled by the children to show the shapes found in them.

INTEGRATING WITH THE REAL WORLD

SHAPE FACE WORKSHEET

skills: naming shapes
finding areas of shapes
drawing shapes

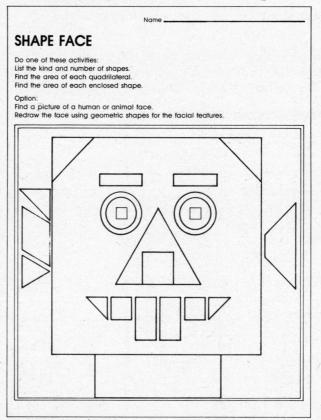

Reproducible, page 148.
Solution, page 194.

GEOMETRY IN ART

skill: researching geometric art

Children research and describe pictures that contain geometric shapes, and report on artists who use geometric shapes as the basis of their style.

RECORD-KEEPING WORKSHEET

WORD FAMILIES/RHYMING WORDS

1. Present words from the various word families for children to read.

2. Dictate words from the various word families for children to spell.

STUDENTS' NAMES	1. CAN READ																2. CAN SPELL															
	at	it	an	ight	ate	ought	able	ack	ong	eet	ake	ouse	ook	ain	ee	ore	at	it	an	ight	ate	ought	able	ack	ong	eet	ake	ouse	ook	ain	ee	ore

Reproducible, page 149.

SKILLS IN THIS SECTION INCLUDE:

- combining consonants and blends with word parts to make words
- developing sound/spelling word families
- reading words in word families
- seeing variations in spelling patterns of rhyming words

Word Families/Rhyming Words

GENERAL ACTIVITIES

TAKE A TURN

skill: combining beginning consonants and blends with word parts to make words

Write a word part on a paper tube. Make a paper ring to slip over the end of the tube. On the ring write consonants and blends that can be added to the word part to make words.

Variation:
Children use words from the tubes in sentences, stories, titles, and other language-arts projects.

1. Turn the ring to make a word.
2. Write down any real words you make.

JACK AND THE BEANSTALK

skill: practicing reading words in various word families

Cut out a large beanstalk for the bulletin board or draw one on the chalkboard.

Variation:
After reaching the top, children get beans from Jack to grow real beanstalks or make paper beanstalks of new words for others to "climb."

1. Climb the beanstalk by reading the words to someone who knows them.
2. When you reach the top, write your name on a golden egg.

WORD-FAMILY EQUATIONS

skills: combining beginning consonants and blends with word parts to make words
alphabetizing
spelling

Explain to the children that the numbers in the equation represent letters according to their order in the alphabet (2 = B, for example).

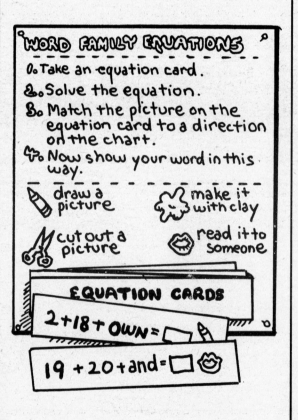

WORD FAMILY EQUATIONS

1. Take an equation card.
2. Solve the equation.
3. Match the picture on the equation card to a direction on the chart.
4. Now show your word in this way.

- draw a picture
- make it with clay
- cut out a picture
- read it to someone

EQUATION CARDS

2 + 18 + OWN =

19 + 20 + and =

GENERAL ACTIVITIES

THE ITY CITY AND ITY CITY WORKSHEET

skills: developing sound/spelling word families
practicing reading words in word families
writing rhyming poetry
comparing rhyming sounds with different spellings

Draw the Ity City on the chalkboard or paper or mount cutouts on a bulletin board. Make a sign for one or more of the following activities:

1. Add words to Ity City.
   a. Write words on the things in Ity City.
   b. Trace around something in Ity City. Add words to what you've made.
   c. Start a booklet or mural of your own Ity City things.
   d. Add a new thing (such as the "ile" smile or the "ack" sack) to Ity City for other children to write words on.
   e. Find words that rhyme with Ity City things but whose rhyming part is spelled differently. Write these words on the back of the Ity City thing ("beat" would be written on the back of "eet-street").
2. Learn and use words from the completed Ity City.
   a. Choose an Ity City thing and learn all the words written on it. Write your initials on any word list you learn.
   b. Write a poem about a thing in Ity City, using all the words written on it.
   c. Color in any thing on your Ity City worksheet whose words you have learned.

Reproducible, page 150.
Solution, page 195.

BLANKETY-BLANK-BLANK WORKSHEET

skills: using rhyming words in poems
writing limericks

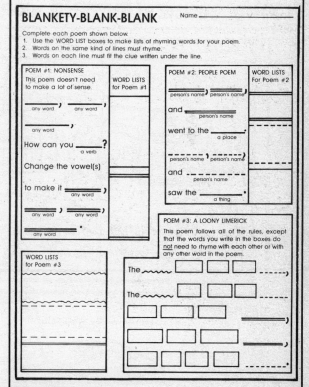

Reproducible, page 151.
Solution, page 195.

LEARNING CENTER

Window areas can provide wall space for charts on which the children can write or for games and activities that have manipulative parts, as well as space where things can be taped or clipped up.

GROUP WORK

FAMILY CIRCLE

*skills: developing word families/rhyming words orally
practicing recall of a series of words
discovering variations in the spelling patterns of rhyming words*

Children sit in a circle. Begin the Family Circle by saying a word from a word family such as "game." The first child in the circle says a word that rhymes with it. The next child repeats the first word, then adds a new word in the same sound family, and so on around the circle.

Variation:
As children name new words, write them on a piece of paper. When the circle is finished with one word family, show the words to the group and discuss them, noting similarities and differences in spelling.

WORD-FAMILY LADDERS

*skills: developing words of increasing length
from a beginning word part
using word parts to aid in spelling*

Draw ladders on paper or the chalkboard. Number each rung of the ladder from bottom to top. On the bottom rung of each ladder write a different word part. Children take turns "climbing" the ladder by writing words that use the original part, each time adding one more letter.

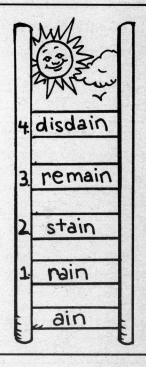

COLOR RHYMES AND RIDDLES

*skills: developing words that
rhyme with color
words
creating riddles*

Pass out a different crayon to each child in the group, and ask children to use the color name of their crayons to make up rhyming phrases, such as "the green bean." Others in the group make up riddles that could be answered by the rhyming phrases.

INDEPENDENT STUDY

RHYMING FACTS AND REASONS

*skills: writing rhyming
couplets
researching*

Have children express researched information in rhyming couplets. Both lines of the couplet may be factual, or one may be a fact while the other is an opinion or imaginary statement related to the fact.

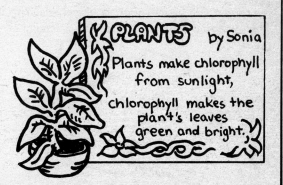

INDEPENDENT STUDY

INTEGRATING WITH THE REAL WORLD

ABC RHYME BOOKS

skills: using rhyming words in writing
alphabetizing
combining letters and word parts to make words

Children use the alphabet and word parts to develop a book of rhymes. The first word (not counting articles) and the last word of each line must rhyme. Each subsequent line of the book must begin with a word starting with the next letter in the alphabet.

TWO-SYLLABLE FAMILIES

skill: developing word families based on two-syllable word parts

Children find or think of words that use the word part you have written on the charts. They then write in these words, making a family.

WORD-FAMILY COLLAGE

skill: developing and illustrating words in a word family
making collages

Children select a word family and collect pictures and words that belong in the family to use in making a collage.

LOOK BOOKS

skill: using real objects to generate rhyming words

Each child takes a piece of paper to any location and draws five objects seen there. Using these pictures as their worksheets, the children draw other objects within the same word family on or next to their original drawings. They then label or write sentences about their pictures. Collect and staple all the papers together to form a Look Book.

ASSESSMENT WORKSHEET

Name _____

VOWELS TEST

To the teacher:
Any or all sections may be used, depending on the skills to be evaluated. Responses may be oral and recorded by teacher or aide, or children may write responses according to directions in each section.

A

Say the name of the picture. Write the vowel you hear next to each picture.

B

Say the word. Write the vowel you hear next to each word.

hit _____   knee _____

hate _____   mop _____

foe _____   gum _____

use _____   ice _____

clap _____   bed _____

C

Say the name of each picture. Use different colored crayons or different numbers to show which pictures have the same vowel sound.

D

Read each list of words. Draw a line between each pair of words that have the same vowel sound.

1	2
shirt	plow
day	bought
ouch	Bert
flaw	soil
look	could
toy	cute
few	steer
toad	soul
thread	said
ear	weigh

Reproducible, page 152.
Solution, page 195.

SKILLS IN THIS SECTION INCLUDE:

- identifying vowel sounds
- developing understanding of diacritical marks
- auditory discrimination of vowel sounds
- matching vowel sounds to key words
- applying vowel rules in writing and pronouncing words
- locating words that do not follow vowel rules

GENERAL ACTIVITIES

ANATOMY OF A VOWEL WORKSHEET

skill: locating words with the same sound/same
spelling pattern to match key words

Variation:

Children list words that have the same sound/
different spelling pattern as the words labeled
on each body part or words that have the same
spelling pattern but a different sound.

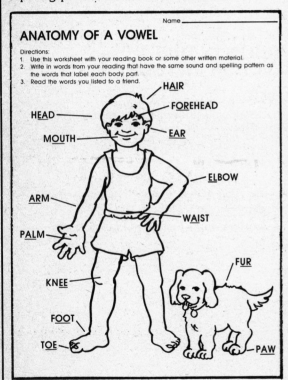

ANATOMY OF A VOWEL

Name_____

Directions:
1. Use this worksheet with your reading book or some other written material.
2. Write in words from your reading that have the same sound and spelling pattern as the words that label each body part.
3. Read the words you listed to a friend.

HAIR
FOREHEAD
HEAD
MOUTH
EAR
ELBOW
ARM
WAIST
PALM
FUR
KNEE
FOOT
TOE
PAW

Reproducible, page 153.
Solution, page 195.

DON'T BE SO SILLY, MILLIE

skills: matching diacritical marks to vowel
sounds in words
applying knowledge of diacritical marks

Use the diacritical marks from a standard dictionary to make a set of cards.

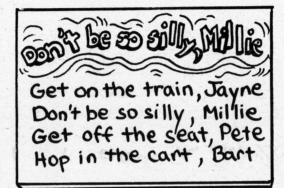

Don't be so silly, Millie

Get on the train, Jayne
Don't be so silly, Millie
Get off the seat, Pete
Hop in the cart, Bart

1. Take a card and match it to the last two words of a line.
2. Write a new line based on the marks on your card.

NEW ADDITIONS TO THE DICTIONARY WORKSHEET

skills: applying vowel rules to pronounce words
using diacritical marks for long, short, and
silent vowels
making up definitions for nonsense words

NEW ADDITIONS TO THE DICTIONARY

Name_____

Follow the directions at the top of each column to complete the worksheet.

Use these marks to show the sounds of the vowels in the words below: ‾ long ˘ short ✕ silent	Write a real word that has the same vowel sound	Make up a definition for the "new" word	Use the "new" word in a sentence to show its meaning
pote			
shay			
chep			
lieg			
dup			
swaip			
bife			
teap			
com			
fleem			
loak			
dind			

Reproducible, page 154.
Solution, page 196.

GENERAL ACTIVITIES

NOAH'S ARK

skills: classifying vowel sounds of pictures and words
auditory discrimination of vowel sounds

To make this activity self-correcting, write numbers or letters on the backs of the cards and provide an answer key. Some other animals that may want to board the ark are aardvarks, pandas, and loons.

VOWELS BAD GUY

skill: locating words that do not follow vowel rules

Children fill out a citation for any word they find in which the vowels do not follow the usual pronunciation rules. Discuss these words with the group and use them in reading, writing, or spelling activities.

LEARNING CENTER

Boxes can be used for storing and displaying center materials. They can be moved to the area where they are to be used and stored easily when not in use.

GROUP WORK

IT'S A SCREAM

*skills: auditory recognition of vowel sounds
    developing sentences*

Draw several speaker's bubbles on the chalkboard or large paper. Elicit exclamatory expressions such as "ow," "eek," and "oo-oo" from the children and write them inside the bubbles. Children name and draw real or imaginary characters to represent each vowel sound contained in these words. Together or alone, other children make up a sentence for each character, using as many words with the same vowel sound as possible.

Variation:
Make the bubbles of construction paper. Children find words from materials read individually or with a group and write them in the appropriate bubbles, which may be displayed for word-study and writing activities.

VOWEL SPELLINGS

*skills: developing word lists based on various vowel sounds
    categorizing words according to vowel sound/spelling patterns*

On the chalkboard or on charts, list any vowel sounds being studied. Discuss each sound. Then ask the group to volunteer words that contain these sounds. List them in any order under the corresponding headings. After many words are listed, ask the children to begin to group them according to the letters used to spell the vowel sounds and to note unusual or less common spellings. Use the word lists in reading, writing, and spelling activities to reinforce knowledge of vowel sound/spelling patterns.

ō				ā			
bow	toe	coke	joke	pay	raid	lane	ray
boat	row	goal	dough	sleigh	face	maid	
soak	doe			cake	weigh	trade	

INDEPENDENT STUDY

JACKET DESIGNING

*skills: auditory recognition and categorization of vowels
    locating key words*

Provide patterns for paper jackets or encourage children to bring in old jackets to decorate. Children collect key words from their independent study and group them according to vowel sounds. Then they design an emblem for each vowel group and list the corresponding key words on it. After the emblems are attached, the children can wear the jackets to share information about their independent study topics. The finished jackets can be used in small-group settings to provide words for auditory-discrimination games with vowel sounds.

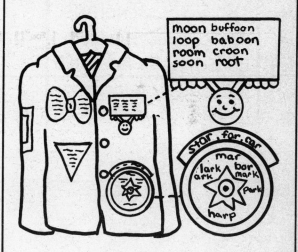

INDEPENDENT STUDY

INTEGRATING WITH THE REAL WORLD

CREATIVE MATCH-UPS

*skills: identifying and matching vowel sounds
        writing creative stories*

Children pair up as independent study partners. They list words from their own independent studies on opposite sides of a sheet of paper. Together the two children draw lines to connect the key words from their studies that have the same vowel sounds or spelling patterns. They then use the connected word pairs in a collaborative creative story.

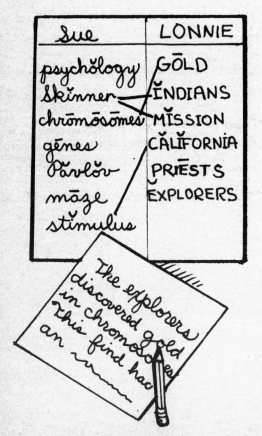

VOWELS CARD GAME

*skills: matching vowel sounds of pictures to key
        words
        column addition*

Collect playing cards from many different decks. Make a gameboard with key words for each vowel being studied and spaces for discards.

FILL-UP STATION

*skill: sorting objects with long and short vowel
       sounds*

Gather real objects and pictures that contain the vowel sounds you are teaching. Some ideas for containers are a tub, can, mitt, and pie pan. To make the activity self-correcting, number all the objects and pictures and provide a key.

ASSESSMENT WORKSHEET

WRITING SENTENCES

Have each student write sentences in WRITING SAMPLE/PRE-TEST, or attach sample sentences from his or her work. Enter comments below. After instruction and practice, repeat for the WRITING SAMPLE/POST-TEST.

Student's Name _____

WRITING SAMPLE/PRE-TEST

Date _____

WRITING SAMPLE/POST-TEST

Date _____

CHECKLIST

Items	Comments/Pre-Test	Comments/Post-Test
Fragments		
Run-ons		
Vocabulary Interesting adjectives, adverbs		
Interesting verbs (uses synonyms for such words as "said," "ran," etc.)		
Other		

Reproducible, page 197.

SKILLS IN THIS SECTION INCLUDE:

- writing different kinds of sentences
- writing descriptive sentences
- identifying and correcting sentence fragments, run-ons, improper word order, and repetitive word usage
- understanding how word order affects sentence meaning

Writing Sentences

GENERAL ACTIVITIES

"SENTENCING"

skill: writing different kinds of sentences

Each task card lists the number of words to use in writing a certain type of sentence.

SENTENCE FRAGMENTS/PICTURE FRAGMENTS WORKSHEET

skill: completing sentence fragments

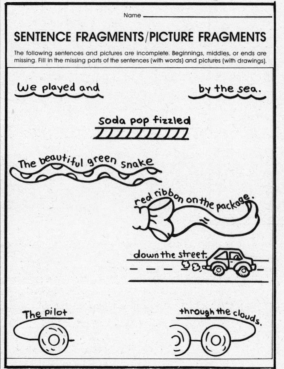

Reproducible, page 156.
Solution, page 196.

REARRANGING SENTENCES WORKSHEET

skill: understanding how word order affects sentence meaning

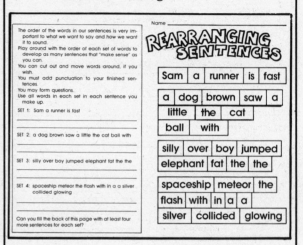

Reproducible, page 157.
Solution, page 196.

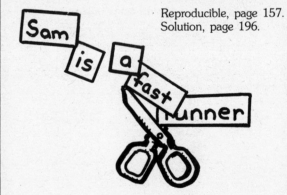

GENERAL ACTIVITIES

SENTENCE EXPANDER WORKSHEET

skill: writing descriptive sentences

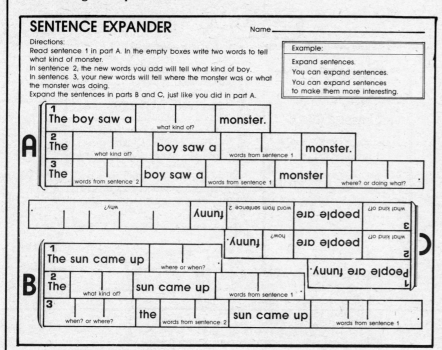

SENTENCE EXPANDER   Name_____

Directions:
Read sentence 1 in part A. In the empty boxes write two words to tell
what kind of monster.
In sentence 2, the new words you add will tell what kind of boy.
In sentence 3, your new words will tell where the monster was or what
the monster was doing.
Expand the sentences in parts B and C, just like you did in part A.

Example:

Expand sentences.
You can expand sentences.
You can expand sentences
to make them more interesting.

A

1 The boy saw a ___ what kind of? ___ monster.

2 The ___ what kind of? ___ boy saw a ___ words from sentence 1 ___ monster.

3 The ___ words from sentence 2 ___ boy saw a ___ words from sentence 1 ___ monster ___ where? or doing what?

(upside down section)
3 people are ___ what kind of? ___ funny ___ word from sentence 2 ___ why? .

2 people are ___ what kind of? ___ funny, ___ how? .

1 People are funny.

B

1 The sun came up ___ where or when? .

2 The ___ what kind of? ___ sun came up ___ words from sentence 1 .

3 ___ when? or where? ___ the ___ words from sentence 2 ___ sun came up ___ words from sentence 1 .

Reproducible, page 158.
Solution, page 196.

SENTENCE SOLVERS

skill: identifying and correcting sentence fragments, run-ons, and improper word order

Write moves on labels and attach them to any game-board. Make a set of cards with various types of sentence problems.

Variation:
For a general review, stack problem cards in EASY and DIFFICULT piles. A card chosen from the DIFFICULT pile and successfully corrected allows children twice as many moves as indicated on the board space.

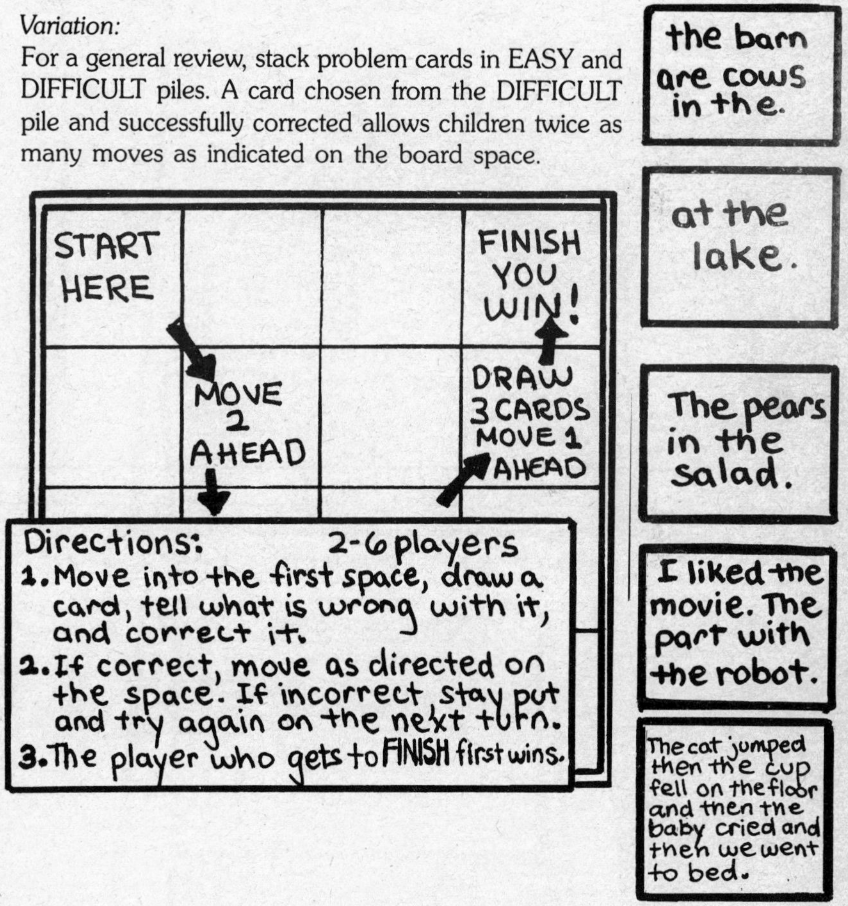

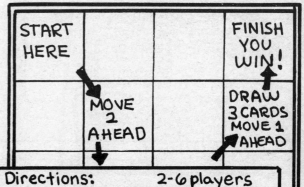

START HERE			FINISH YOU WIN!
			DRAW 3 CARDS MOVE 1 AHEAD
	MOVE 2 AHEAD		

Directions: 2-6 players
1. Move into the first space, draw a card, tell what is wrong with it, and correct it.
2. If correct, move as directed on the space. If incorrect stay put and try again on the next turn.
3. The player who gets to FINISH first wins.

the barn are cows in the.

at the lake.

The pears in the salad.

I liked the movie. The part with the robot.

The cat jumped then the cup fell on the floor and then the baby cried and then we went to bed.

LEARNING CENTER

Easels provide a two-sided bulletin board on which to display center materials. They can be moved to convenient spots in or out of the classroom.

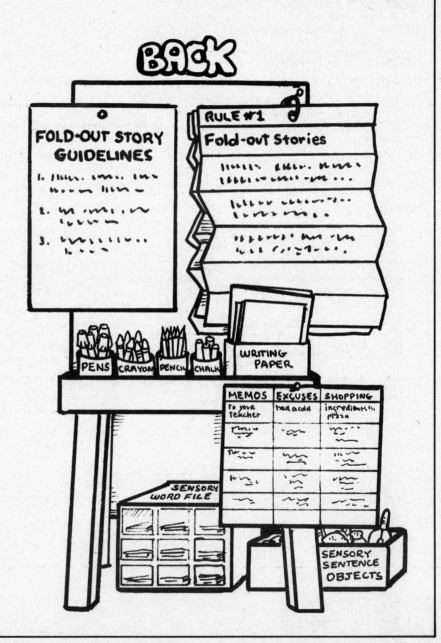

GROUP WORK

FOLD-OUT STORY

skills: writing sentences to complete a cooperative story
avoiding sentence "pitfalls" such as uninteresting sentences or repetitive word usage

Write the first sentence for a story on the top fold of a large piece of paper. Children continue the story by dictating or writing additional sentences on each fold. As a reference in constructing the story, devise a guideline or select one from a prepared chart.

> RULE #1
>
> John had an awful nightmare.
>
> In his dream he could only say two words.
>
> These two words were bye, bye.
>
> No one understood what little Johnny meant.
>
> But his sister understood him.

Variation:
The group may write the story before discussing guidelines. Then they edit the story according to given guidelines or ones developed by the group.

Fold-out story guidelines   by Group 2
1. Proper names must be repeated only once (i.e.: "John" must later be replaced by "he," "the boy," etc.).
2. "And," "then," "because" and "so" may each be used only once to begin a sentence.
3. Each adjective may be used only once.
4. Each noun must be described by an adjective.
5. More descriptive adjectives must be used in place of such words as big, little, very (i.e.: "big ball" becomes "enormous ball").
6. Select more exciting verbs to use instead of went, gone, walk, said, etc.

MANY-ANSWERS MINIBOARDS

skill: writing complete sentences to answer a question

Provide children with paper, small chalkboards, or space at the classroom chalkboard. Ask a question to which children orally volunteer complete-sentence answers. Then ask another question and have students write their own answer to it on their papers or chalkboards. Compare the written answers and evaluate them in terms of completeness, while noting the variety of ways for stating the same or similar answers.

INDEPENDENT STUDY

ONE-LINERS

skill: rewriting sentences while maintaining original meanings

Write famous one-line quotes at the tops of different charts. Children select a quote and rewrite it, using their own words but retaining the original meaning of the quote. Add each rendition of the quote to the chart so that other students can read, compare, and discuss the sentences.

"I NEVER MET A MAN I DIDN'T LIKE." WILL ROGERS

"GIVE ME LIBERTY OR GIVE ME DEATH" — Patrick Henry
I'd rather die than lose my freedom — Gail
Let me have a stilled heart before a stilled voice — Joe

INTEGRATING WITH THE REAL WORLD

SENSORY SENTENCES

skills: using the five senses in developing descriptive writing
vocabulary building

Collect objects that appeal to the senses. Label the compartments of liquor boxes with the names of the objects.

DIRECTIONS:
1. Choose an object, examine it with your senses, and write words to describe it on cards.
2. Use your descriptive words in sentences about the object.
3. File your cards in the box.

DIRECTIONS:
1. Choose
2. Use
3. File

SILK
SALT
BELL

Tim
The clear, glass bell felt cool to the touch. It gave out a shimmery

shimmery

clear

SENTENCES, PLEASE

skill: translating oral communication, lists, and phrases into sentences

Make a chart or worksheet, with the children's help, of many situations in which writing or oral reporting is needed. Children choose one or more of the situations to use for a given time period—a day, week, or month. Whenever their situations occur, the children must write the communication in sentence form rather than telling someone or writing phrases or word lists.

MEMOS	EXCUSES	SHOPPING
to your teacher	had a cold	ingredients for pizza
to yourself	went to dentist	ingredients for spaghetti
to parents about what's happening in school	on vacation	supplies for your birthday party
	overslept	new clothes

Spaghetti List   Grace
I need tomato sauce and paste. I think I'll get vermicelli. I'll check the prices on Italian sausage and ground meat.

ASSESSMENT WORKSHEET

PUNCTUATION POWER

DIFFICULT

7. Pardon me Peter Piper said I need to put my peppers here

6. Peter Pipers pockets were full of picked pickled peppers

5. Help me pick peppers said Peter Piper

4. Peter also picked potatoes peas petunias parsley and pears

3. Fantastic Forty-two pecks of peppers

2. How many pecks did Peter Piper pick

1. Peter Piper picked a peck of pickled peppers

EASY

Directions:
Punctuate each sentence, from easy to difficult. Color in the scale to show your punctuation power.

Name_____

Reproducible, page 159.
Solution, page 197.

SKILLS IN THIS SECTION INCLUDE:

- using correct punctuation in different contexts
- practicing proofreading skills
- using capitals

Punctuation

GENERAL ACTIVITIES

PUNCTUATION PARADIGMS

skill: using punctuation in sentences, stories, and poems

Children select or are assigned a task card. An area for storing work and a simple recording worksheet or chart of names can be provided.

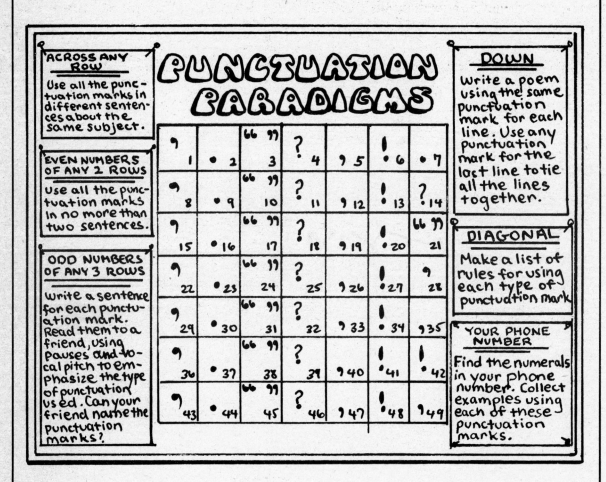

ACROSS ANY ROW
Use all the punctuation marks in different sentences about the same subject.

EVEN NUMBERS OF ANY 2 ROWS
Use all the punctuation marks in no more than two sentences.

ODD NUMBERS OF ANY 3 ROWS
Write a sentence for each punctuation mark. Read them to a friend, using pauses and vocal pitch to emphasize the type of punctuation used. Can your friend name the punctuation marks?

DOWN
Write a poem using the same punctuation mark for each line. Use any punctuation mark for the last line to tie all the lines together.

DIAGONAL
Make a list of rules for using each type of punctuation mark

YOUR PHONE NUMBER
Find the numerals in your phone number. Collect examples using each of these punctuation marks.

STAND-UP SENTENCES

skill: using capitals

Children read a sentence strip and determine whether a capital or lower-case letter is needed at the beginning of each word. They hang the appropriate side of the letter card over the word to show their choice. The students can correct their answers by locating the alliterative letter used in the strip on an alphabetized answer sheet and reading the corrected sentence.

GENERAL ACTIVITIES

PUNCTUATION PATTERNS WORKSHEET

*skill: writing sentences following
punctuation patterns*

Name_____

PUNCTUATION PATTERNS

Fill in the blanks with words to make sentences that use the punctuation marks correctly.

1. _____

   _____ , _____ . _____ _____ _____

2. _____ ?

3. " _____ "

4. _____

5. _____ !

6. _____ " _____ "

   _____ ? "

7. " _____

   _____ ? "

8. _____ , _____ _____

   _____ , _____ _____

   _____ "

9. _____

10. _____ ! _____ ! _____ !

Reproducible, page 160.
Solution, page 197.

PUNCTUATION PINS

skill: punctuating sentences

Variation:
Children working in small groups can race each other by using the same set of sentence strips and their own sets of punctuation pins.

BOTHERSOME BUGS WORKSHEET

*skill: using colons, semicolons, dashes, and
parentheses*

Name_____

BOTHERSOME BUGS

DIRECTIONS
Cut out the bug body parts.
Match the bug body parts to form complete sentences.
Glue completed bugs on a piece of paper.
Make up some of your own bothersome bugs,
using the same punctuation marks.

The ocean liner set sail for France

France, Germany, and Greece.

I won't say.

I don't know

We visited the following countries

however, hostile natives forced it back to port.

see the enclosed photo

and can travel a long way without water.

The camels in Egypt have two humps

Reproducible, page 161.
Solution, page 197.

LEARNING CENTER

A table next to a bulletin board or wall is an easy, convenient way to set up a learning center without making major changes in the classroom's basic seating arrangement.

GROUP WORK

PROOFREADER'S PANEL

skill: punctuating oral and written sentences

After the sentence is presented, group members write the sentence with the punctuation mark they feel is necessary and hold up their responses for the author of the sentence to see.

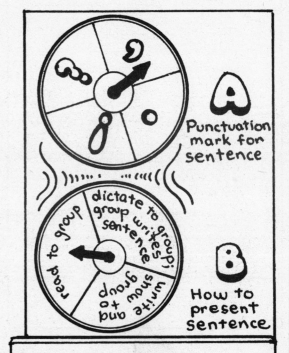

A Punctuation mark for sentence

B How to present sentence

1. Spin both spinners.
2. Make up a sentence with the punctuation mark from wheel A.
3. Present your sentence as shown on wheel B.

GROUP WORK

COLORFUL CORRECTING

skill: proofreading unpunctuated material

Make a color wheel on which you include any punctuation rules appropriate to what your children have learned. Prepare a chart or worksheets with unpunctuated text. Each child or group chooses a section and proofreads the text. The color-coded copy is a record of their work and becomes the basis for group discussions.

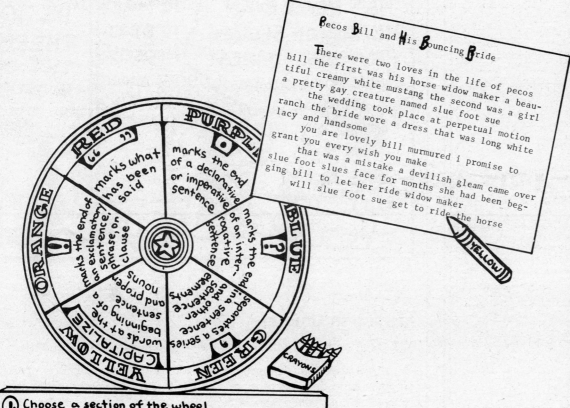

Pecos Bill and His Bouncing Bride

There were two loves in the life of pecos bill the first was his horse widow maker a beautiful creamy white mustang the second was a girl a pretty gay creature named slue foot sue the wedding took place at perpetual motion ranch the bride wore a dress that was long white lacy and handsome
you are lovely bill murmured i promise to grant you every wish you make
that was a mistake a devilish gleam came over slue foot slues face for months she had been begging bill to let her ride widow maker
will slue foot sue get to ride the horse

Color wheel sections:
- **RED** — marks what has been said
- **PURPLE** — marks the end of a declarative or imperative sentence
- **ORANGE** — marks the end of an exclamatory sentence, or phrase, or clause
- **BLUE** — marks the end of an interrogative sentence
- **GREEN** — separates a series and other sentence elements
- **YELLOW** — CAPITALIZE words at the beginning of a sentence and proper nouns

1. Choose a section of the wheel.
2. Follow the rule on your section of the wheel as you proofread the text. Use the same color pen, pencil, or crayon as your section.
3. Continue with each color of the wheel.

INDEPENDENT STUDY

TIME CAPSULE PUNCTUATION WORKSHEET

skills: proofreading for punctuation marks and capital letters
researching

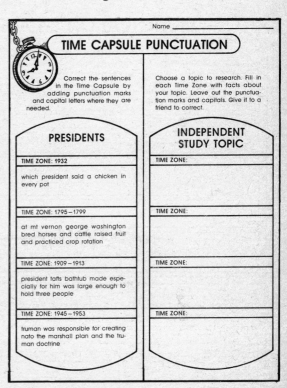

Name _____

TIME CAPSULE PUNCTUATION

Correct the sentences in the Time Capsule by adding punctuation marks and capital letters where they are needed.

Choose a topic to research. Fill in each Time Zone with facts about your topic. Leave out the punctuation marks and capitals. Give it to a friend to correct.

PRESIDENTS	INDEPENDENT STUDY TOPIC
TIME ZONE: 1932	TIME ZONE:
which president said a chicken in every pot	
TIME ZONE: 1795–1799	TIME ZONE:
at mt vernon george washington bred horses and cattle raised fruit and practiced crop rotation	
TIME ZONE: 1909–1913	TIME ZONE:
president tafts bathtub made especially for him was large enough to hold three people	
TIME ZONE: 1945–1953	TIME ZONE:
truman was responsible for creating nato the marshall plan and the truman doctrine	

Reproducible, page 162.
Solution, page 197.

INTEGRATING WITH THE REAL WORLD

PUNCTUATION P's AND Q's WORKSHEET

skill: putting together punctuation marks and words to form sentences

---

Name _____

PUNCTUATION P's AND Q's

Use the punctuation marks and words to make sentences. Add any other words or punctuation marks you need.

? .	problem popular queer	_____
! ,	quit phone poor	_____
. " "	quiver quake prince	_____
? ,	purple quart	_____
. !	quarantine queen parrot	_____

Write your initials here: _____

Fill in each box with words that begin with your initials. Use the punctuation marks and words to make sentences. Add any other words or punctuation marks you need.

? " " . ___	_____
. , . ___	_____
, . ___	_____
! ! ? ___	_____
" " , . ___	_____

Reproducible, page 163.
Solution, page 198.

COMIC STRIPS

skills: using quotation marks
    identifying direct quotations and the speakers

Collect comic strips from magazines and newspapers. Children add (1) quotation marks and any other necessary punctuation to a comic strip to indicate what is being said and (2) phrases to indicate who is speaking.

NEWSPAPER ARTICLES

skill: applying rules for the correct usage of punctuation and capitals

Cut out articles from newspapers or children's magazines. Children paste an article onto one side of a piece of paper and circle and number each capital and punctuation mark in the article. On the other side of the paper, they write the number of the capital or punctuation mark and why it was used in the article. If they find any typographical errors in punctuation, they should make corrections and explain them. Children can act as proof-readers for each other.

ASSESSMENT WORKSHEET

PARTS OF SPEECH

To the teacher:
Write in an appropriate sentence.

DIAGNOSTIC SENTENCE: _____

Have each student read the sentence. Then ask the child to point out a noun, tell what a noun does, and give several examples of other nouns. Check for understanding of other parts of speech in the same manner.

STUDENTS' NAMES	DATE	NOUN			ADJECTIVE			VERB			ADVERB			OTHER		
		Identifies in context	Defines purpose	Gives new examples	Identifies in context	Defines purpose	Gives new examples	Identifies in context	Defines purpose	Gives new examples	Identifies in context	Defines purpose	Gives new examples	Identifies in context	Defines purpose	Gives new examples

Reproducible, page 164.

SKILLS IN THIS SECTION INCLUDE:

- identifying types of nouns, adjectives, verbs, and adverbs
- identifying and using nouns, adjectives, verbs, and adverbs in different contexts

Parts of Speech

GENERAL ACTIVITIES

USE YOUR NAME WORKSHEET

skill: writing examples of nouns, adjectives, verbs, and adverbs in categories

Variation:
Make this activity into a reading followup by writing the name of a story character in the boxes at the top of the worksheet. Children fill in the columns with words from the story or words that relate to the story.

USE YOUR NAME   Name _____

Directions:
1. Spell out your name in the boxes across the top.
2. Under each letter, write parts of speech that begin with that letter. Use adjectives that modify the nouns and adverbs that modify the verbs you've written for each letter.
3. Write a sentence for each group of words in a column. You will need to add other words and punctuation.

NOUN						
ADJECTIVE						
VERB						
ADVERB						

Reproducible, page 165.
Solution, page 198.

PARTS-OF-SPEECH POETRY

skill: using nouns, verbs, adjectives, and adverbs in context

Children follow poetry-formula cards to create rhyming or nonrhyming poems. Other children may try to match the poems to the formulas from which they were written.

PARTS-OF-SPEECH DOMINOES WORKSHEET

skills: matching nouns, adjectives, verbs, and adverbs
giving examples of nouns, verbs, adjectives, and adverbs

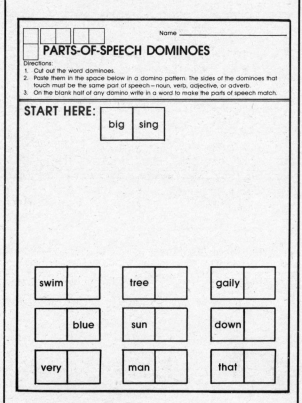

Reproducible, page 166.
Solution, page 198.

GENERAL ACTIVITIES

SLIDING SENTENCE STRIPS

skill: matching adjectives, verbs, and adverbs for consistency of meaning

Children move the word strips through the windows in the sentence strips to find a combination of words that make sense. They write down all the sentences they make.

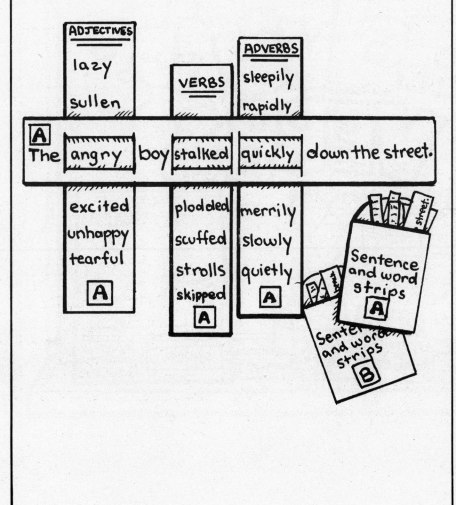

PARTS-OF-SPEECH CHARACTERS

skills: identifying nouns, verbs, adjectives, and adverbs
identifying types of nouns, verbs, adjectives, and adverbs

Variation:
Children sort the words from one part of speech category (such as Adjectives) into subcategories (such as Descriptive or Limiting).

LEARNING CENTER

A portion of the chalkboard makes a good space for activities that require the children to write, and for things that may need to be changed or are not necessary to keep for later use. The chalk railing can be used to display other center materials.

GROUP WORK

GROUP WRITING

skill: replacing nouns, adjectives, verbs, and adverbs in sentences

Write a simple sentence on a chart or chalkboard. Children select or are assigned parts of speech—noun, adjective, verb, or adverb. Reread the sentence and have the children substitute synonyms for any word that is "their" part of speech. They try to replace words as many times as possible while maintaining the general meaning of the original sentence.

Variation:

Begin a story. Have the children add to the story, assuming the roles of various parts of speech. For example, a child wearing the noun sign responds with an appropriate noun for the story when you ask for one.

wee maid ran
tiny gal moved rapidly market
small lass proceeded swiftly shop
The little girl went quickly to the store.

GEOMETRIC ADD-ONS

skill: generating adjectives, verbs, and adverbs for a given noun

Draw a geometric shape on a chart or chalkboard. Write a common noun in the strip. Draw a larger outline of the first shape and ask children to think of adjectives to modify the noun. Write an adjective on each line segment of the geometric shape. Continue adding larger shapes for other parts of speech—verbs to describe the function or use of the noun and adverbs to modify each verb. Have children make up sentences combining the parts of speech.

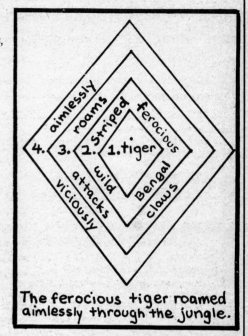

The ferocious tiger roamed aimlessly through the jungle.

ADJECTIVES CHART

skill: naming descriptive and limiting adjectives

Select one of the types of adjectives shown on the chart. Then one of the students takes a noun card and responds with an example of the type of adjective selected. The same noun card may be used for all the other types of adjectives, or a new card may be drawn for each new type of adjective selected.

INDEPENDENT STUDY

INDEPENDENT STUDY COLLECTORS

*skills: identifying nouns and verbs
        taking notes*

This activity will stimulate children to find information in a given area in depth and encourage them to take notes and develop skill in report writing.

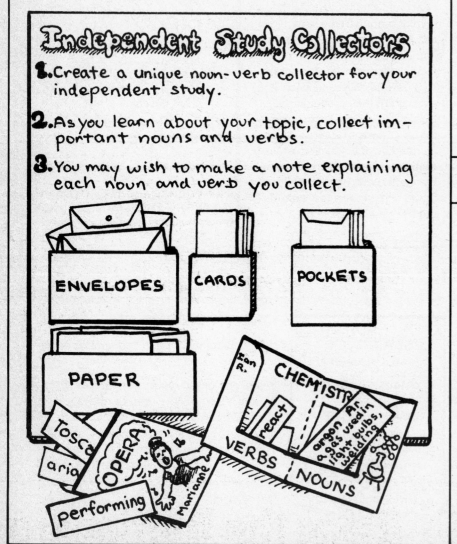

PICTURE LABELS

*skills: labeling nouns, adjectives,
        verbs, and adverbs related
        to a picture*

Collect pictures from magazines and posters related to the children's independent studies. Using marking pens or crayons, children label the nouns in the pictures. Then they fill in adjectives to describe the nouns they have labeled. They also write in verbs to label actions seen or inferred in the picture and adverbs to describe these verbs. The pictures can be a basis for creative writing.

INTEGRATING WITH THE REAL WORLD

PROPER-NOUN FILES

*skills: naming and writing proper nouns
        classifying
        alphabetizing*

The file boxes can be a resource for creative writing activities or for practice in alphabetizing.

ASSESSMENT WORKSHEET

USING THE DICTIONARY

Name _____

Beginning Time _____

Ending Time _____

MY WORK	TEACHER'S COMMENTS
1. Circle the pair of guide words that would be listed on the page where these words are found. raccoon — rabbit — razor race — reach spaghetti — shell — space smell — string	
2. Look up these words. Write the definition for each. judge _____ suddenly _____ reimburse _____	
3. Divide these words into syllables. habitat _____ peppermint _____ society _____	
4. Rewrite each list in alphabetical order. fig _____ deer _____ pear _____ dog _____ berry _____ dime _____ lemon _____ dozen _____ orange _____ dial _____	
5. Pronounce these words for the teacher. a. kee´-hohl e. pou´-dər b. fayz´ f. pik´-chər c. skip´-r g. mär´-shən d. swahp´ h. ri-dōōs´	

Reproducible, page 167.
Solution, page 198.

SKILLS IN THIS SECTION INCLUDE:

- understanding the parts of a dictionary
- locating words and other information, such as synonyms and spelling, in the dictionary
- recognizing root words and word variations
- extending vocabulary
- understanding diacritical marks

Using the Dictionary

GENERAL ACTIVITIES

WORD-OF-THE-DAY CHART

skills: using context clues
locating words in a dictionary
using new vocabulary

Select a word from a sentence, comic strip, or cartoon and display both the source and the word. When the Definitions Guesses pocket is full, children compare their definitions with the dictionary definition to establish the correct meaning of the word. The previous day's word becomes the word for the Use It the Most Contest. The child who uses this word the most during the day is considered the winner. The words are kept for review and language-arts activities.

RIGHT OR WRONG

skill: using the dictionary to check spelling

Make word cards of correctly and incorrectly spelled words.

1. Each player takes a card.

2. If you think the word is spelled correctly, put in **RIGHT** pocket. If not, put in **WRONG** pocket.

3. Verify the spelling of the words with a dictionary.

4. If you placed the card in the correct pocket, spin the spinner to earn points.

5. The winner will have the highest score tallied during game.

SENSIBLE SYNONYMS WORKSHEET

skills: using the dictionary to find synonyms
developing vocabulary

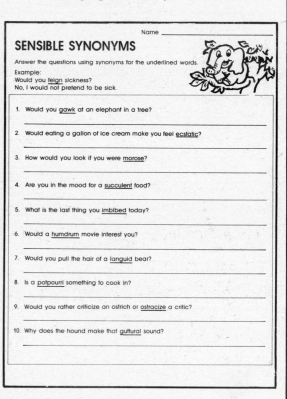

Name _____

SENSIBLE SYNONYMS

Answer the questions using synonyms for the underlined words.
Example:
Would you <u>feign</u> sickness?
No, I would not pretend to be sick.

1. Would you <u>gawk</u> at an elephant in a tree?

2. Would eating a gallon of ice cream make you feel <u>ecstatic</u>?

3. How would you look if you were <u>morose</u>?

4. Are you in the mood for a <u>succulent</u> food?

5. What is the last thing you <u>imbibed</u> today?

6. Would a <u>humdrum</u> movie interest you?

7. Would you pull the hair of a <u>languid</u> bear?

8. Is a <u>potpourri</u> something to cook in?

9. Would you rather criticize an ostrich or <u>ostracize</u> a critic?

10. Why does the hound make that <u>guttural</u> sound?

Reproducible, page 168.
Solution, page 199.

GENERAL ACTIVITIES

GUIDE WORD POCKET CHARTS

skills: using guide words
alphabetizing

1. Choose a chart.

2. Pick word cards that you would find on the same page with the guide words.

3. File in A B C order.

4. Record what you have done. Turn chart over to see if you are correct.

WORDS, WORDS, WORDS WORKSHEET

skills: locating words
recognizing guide words, syllables, and definitions

WORDS, WORDS, WORDS

Each time your shape appears you must fill it in with the information asked for. Some words you might like to use: novel, drone, produce, inducement.

TEAM MEMBERS: ○─_____ □─_____ △─_____

WORD		
GUIDE WORDS		
SYLLABLES		
ONE DEFINITION		

Reproducible, page 169.
Solution, page 199.

DESIGN A DICTIONARY PAGE WORKSHEET

skill: understanding how a dictionary page is set up

Name _____

DESIGN A DICTIONARY PAGE

Directions:
1. Select nine words for your dictionary page.
2. Complete the worksheet by including all the parts used in a dictionary page, such as guide word, entry word, pronunciation, definition, illustration (for one of the words), and part of speech.

Reproducible, page 170.
Solution, page 199.

LEARNING CENTER

A file cabinet or other drawer space (perhaps the teacher's desk) combines the advantages of a compact space with easy accessibility. This method of center display is also a boon to teachers who want their classrooms to be less cluttered and more organized.

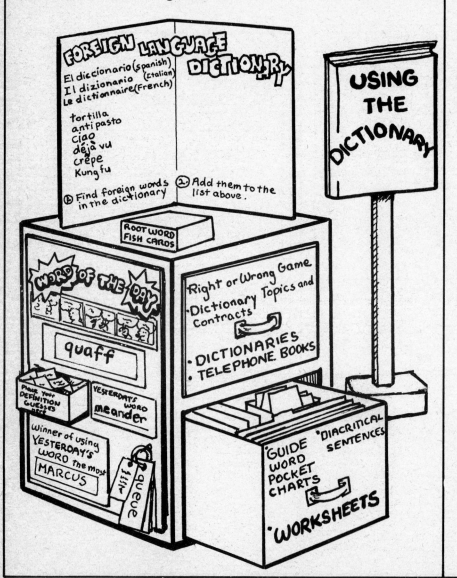

GROUP WORK

DIACRITICAL SENTENCES

skill: decoding diacritically marked words

After practice at decoding teacher-prepared diacritical sentences, children use the dictionary to prepare sentences for others to read.

> Thə bâr went óvər the moun·tən.

> I wil kum tōō yôr hous tə·môr.'ō.

DICTIONARY RACE

skill: locating words in a dictionary

Provide each member of the group with a dictionary. Call out a letter or word. The first child to locate the letter or word in the dictionary is the winner, and may call out the next item to be located by the rest of the group.

TELEPHONE BOOK LOOK

skill: comparing the telephone book with dictionaries

Distribute telephone books and dictionaries to the group members. Guide them in comparing how the telephone book is similar to and different from the dictionary in use and form.

GROUP WORK

INDEPENDENT STUDY

ROOT WORD FISH

skill: matching root words with variant forms

Make four card sets of words with the same roots. The children are dealt cards and play this game using the traditional rules of Go Fish.

BROWSE THROUGH THE DICTIONARY

skill: learning to enjoy the dictionary

Children find unusual or funny words in the dictionary—proper names, abbreviations, long words, foreign words, or illustrated words. The group may keep add-on charts or lists over a period of time.

GREEK AND LATIN VERBAL VIRTUOSITY

skill: learning Greek and Latin roots forming derivative words

Children can also make similar lists of words from their independent study. Science and math are fields that lend themselves to this activity.

THE BIRTH OF A DICTIONARY

skills: researching development of a dictionary sequencing

Draw a sample or have the children design their own flow chart to depict stages in the development of a dictionary. Key words for elements to include and reference books should be available to the students. This chart could also be made into a worksheet for children to complete.

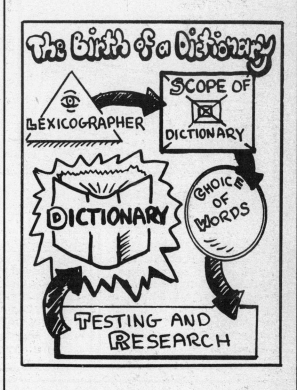

INDEPENDENT STUDY

INTEGRATING WITH THE REAL WORLD

DICTIONARY TOPICS

skills: using special-topic dictionaries
finding and applying prefix and suffix
meanings
researching lexicographers
comparing dictionaries
finding slang in dictionaries

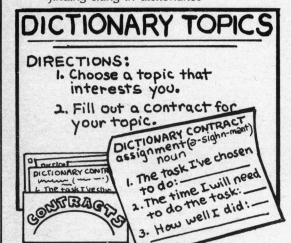

DICTIONARY TOPICS

DIRECTIONS:
1. Choose a topic that interests you.
2. Fill out a contract for your topic.

DICTIONARY CONTRACT
assignment (ə-sighn-mənt)
noun
1. The task I've chosen to do: ___
2. The time I will need to do the task: ___
3. How well I did: ___

TOPICS

WORD DISPLAY:
Use a specialized dictionary written for a specific topic, such as ballet, medicine, or music. Design a display of models, illustrations and/or diagrams to show the meanings of some of the words.

PREFIXES AND SUFFIXES:
Select prefixes and suffixes from this list: -ism, ite, mis-, -ment, dis-, -ful, -eous, -ants. Look up their meanings. Find words using these prefixes and suffixes and define them.

COMPARING DICTIONARIES:
Use two dictionaries with the same copyright date, or two dictionaries with copyright dates that are at least ten years apart. Think of several slang words. Look them up in each dictionary. Describe what makes these words alike and different in each dictionary.

FAMOUS LEXICOGRAPHERS: Research one or more of these men: Funk, Wagnall, Webster. Tell why they are famous.

LOOK-UP BOOK

skill: using a dictionary for vocabulary development

Make or purchase small tablets for children to use to collect words they need to know or would like to look up in the dictionary. Encourage parents to assist children in looking up these words in dictionaries at home.

CROSSWORD PUZZLES

skills: using a dictionary for vocabulary development
making and doing crossword puzzles

Give children crossword puzzles from children's magazines and newspapers. Children can also develop their own crossword puzzles using words from topics of interest or class studies.

NOW NEWS WORDS

skills: making new dictionary pages
vocabulary development

Children develop a dictionary page of words related to current events. Dictionary pages can be designed for newspaper articles, radio and TV newscasts, or special events such as the school's Olympic games.

PRODUCT REWRITES

skills: understanding diacritical marks
using diacritical marks

Ask children to bring in advertisements and labels from products they use. Have them rewrite names or words from these, using dictionary respellings and diacritical marks. Students can do their own rewrites of product names not found in the dictionary by using the pronunciation key's words and diacritical marks.

RECORD-KEEPING WORKSHEET

PREFIXES AND SUFFIXES

Assess the children in a group activity, such as Pass the Hat (page 65), in the following way:

- ▱ not introduced to skill
- ◨ working on the skill
- ■ mastery of the skill

STUDENTS' NAMES	Identifies prefixes in words	Defines prefixes	Gives words containing prefixes	Defines words containing prefixes	Uses words containing prefixes in a sentence	Knows these prefixes:	Identifies suffixes in words	Defines suffixes	Gives words containing suffixes	Defines words containing suffixes	Uses words containing suffixes in a sentence	Knows these suffixes:

Reproducible, page 171.

SKILLS IN THIS SECTION INCLUDE:

- identifying, defining, and using prefixes and suffixes
- using words containing prefixes and suffixes
- combining prefixes and suffixes with root words to make words

Prefixes and Suffixes

GENERAL ACTIVITIES

NUTS AND BOLTS

skill: combining root words, prefixes, and suffixes to make words

Write root words on long strips of chipboard or heavy cardboard. Write prefixes and suffixes on shorter strips. Make holes to fit a selected size of bolt at the top of each of the strips.

PREFIX AND SUFFIX SERVICE, INC., WORKSHEET

skills: making words by combining root words, prefixes, and suffixes

making spelling changes in root words when adding suffixes

PREFIX AND SUFFIX SERVICE, INC.

Directions:
Fill in the top of the worksheet. Use the information in the PART(S) and QUANTITY columns to make words. Write the words in the LABOR column. Note any spelling changes in the SERVICE column.

Date _____

Name _____
Address _____
City _____ State _____ Zip Code _____
Telephone _____

PART(S)	QUANTITY	LABOR	SERVICE
ANCE	2 words		
RE	3 words		
TION	6 words		
UN	4 words		
DIS, LY	5 words		
FUL	2 words		
SUB	3 words		
LESS	5 words		
ENT	2 words		

Reproducible, page 172.
Solution, page 199.

FIX-IT REFERENCE MANUAL

skills: identifying words that have prefixes and suffixes

deriving meanings of words using prefixes and suffixes

using a dictionary to find meanings

using prefix and suffix words in sentences

Title each page of a blank booklet with a prefix or suffix, leaving several pages blank for children to label as they find other prefixes and suffixes. Children add words that contain the prefixes and suffixes, and write a sentence using the word or a phrase describing the word. They may try to determine the definition of a word by studying the meanings of the root word, prefixes, and suffixes or look it up in a dictionary.

GENERAL ACTIVITIES

AT YOUR SERVICE WORKSHEET

skill: using words containing prefixes and suffixes

Name _____

AT YOUR SERVICE

Directions:
1. Write the name of a job or business you would like to have—for example, TV repairperson.
2. On the shapes below, write slogans or ads related to the job you chose, using as many words as you can that have prefixes and suffixes:
3. Underline or circle each prefix or suffix you use.

Fill in your business card, including a slogan and a short description of your business or service.

Write a slogan for your workclothes.

Write a slogan on your badge.

Write a slogan or ad on your truck

Reproducible, page 173.
Solution, page 200.

PREFIX/SUFFIX CROSSWORD WORKSHEET

skills: using words containing prefixes and suffixes
using the meanings of prefixes and suffixes to complete a puzzle

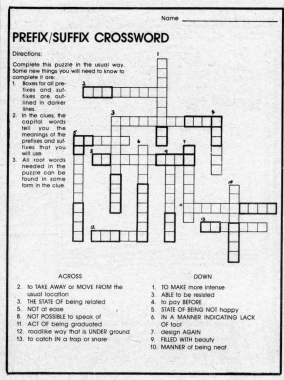

Name _____

PREFIX/SUFFIX CROSSWORD

Directions:

Complete this puzzle in the usual way. Some new things you will need to know to complete it are:
1. Boxes for all prefixes and suffixes are outlined in darker lines.
2. In the clues, the capital words tell you the meanings of the prefixes and suffixes that you will use.
3. All root words needed in the puzzle can be found in some form in the clue.

ACROSS

2. to TAKE AWAY or MOVE FROM the usual location
3. THE STATE OF being related
5. NOT at ease
8. NOT POSSIBLE to speak of
11. ACT OF being graduated
12. roadlike way that is UNDER ground
13. to catch IN a trap or snare

DOWN

1. TO MAKE more intense
3. ABLE to be resisted
4. to pay BEFORE
5. STATE OF BEING NOT happy
6. IN A MANNER INDICATING LACK OF tact
7. design AGAIN
9. FILLED WITH beauty
10. MANNER of being neat

Reproducible, page 174.
Solution, page 200.

PREFIX/SUFFIX TIC-TAC-TOE WORKSHEET

skill: identifying prefixes and suffixes

GAME 1		
sleepless understand uncover	helpful story unaware	outside rearrange partnership
displace exclamation butcher	rechargeable sidewalk unleash	forgetful discontent lumber
enjoyment repair parade	proclaim difference restaurant	snowman painless subhuman

PREFIX/SUFFIX TIC-TAC-TOE

Names _____ (player 1)
_____ (player 2)

Directions:
(2 players)
In each game, decide who will be P and who will be S (flip a coin or draw). P marks prefixes; S marks suffixes. The youngest player begins the game.
1. Choose a square and find the word that contains your word part.
2. Read the word and spell the prefix or suffix.
3. If you are correct, the square is yours and you may mark it. If you are wrong, the square belongs to the other player.
4. Settle any disagreements with a dictionary.

Game 1 Winner _____

Game 2 Winner _____ Game 3 Winner _____

GAME 2				GAME 3		
coexist comfort disappearance	happiness rename purple	plastic decode fulfillment		portion afterward preoccupy	restate fearless toothpaste	action inside retell
cooperate painful product	distaste favorable recognize	reletter cupful relation		parlor kindness preview	bemoan armchair lamentable	playful liquid regain
beside homeward direction	attempt homeless disbelief	return backward jingle		playground undecidedly rejoin	promotion cowboy antifreeze	seasonal sportsmanship interact

Reproducible, page 175.
Solution, page 200.

LEARNING CENTER

This center is an example of blending a topic with a skill area to arrive at a title and theme format. The skill activities are designed around the theme.

GROUP WORK

PASS THE HAT

skills: defining prefixes and suffixes
naming words containing a given prefix or suffix
defining words containing a prefix or suffix

Pass the hat and have four children in the group draw a card. The child with card #1 begins the cycle by choosing a prefix or suffix and giving its definition. The child with card #2 names a word containing that suffix or prefix. The child with card #3 defines the word, and the one with card #4 uses the word in a sentence. While responding, each child takes the hat from the previous person and places his or her card inside. After all four have responded, pass the hat again to four other children.

PREFIX/SUFFIX HANDBALL

skills: naming words using given prefixes and suffixes
practicing ball-bouncing skills

Divide a very large piece of butcher paper into twelve squares. Label each square and tape the chart onto a handball backboard. Children take turns bouncing the ball at the backboard. They note which square the ball hits, catch the ball, and then name a word that uses the prefix or suffix in that square. A correct word earns the number of points shown in the square. The child who earns the most points after several rounds is the winner.

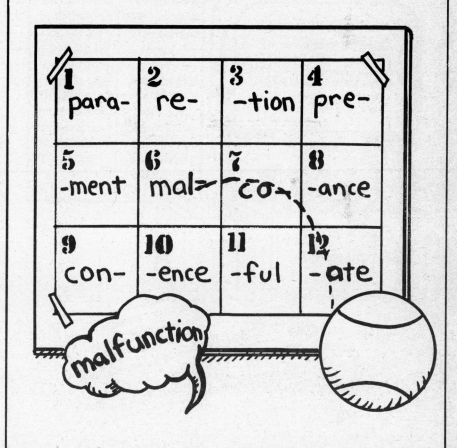

INDEPENDENT STUDY

SMALL APPLIANCE FIX-IT DIRECTIONS

skills: understanding meanings of words that contain prefixes and suffixes
writing directions

Collect diagrams used for assembly, owner-operator manuals, and catalogues that name the parts or describe the workings of appliances. Although the children's repair directions may not be technically correct, they should use words in an appropriate context.

SERVICES RENDERED

dismantle	untangle
disconnect	enlarge
unfasten	replace
rewire	repair
restore	pliable
dislodge	bendable
refinish	entanglement
unscrew	lubrication
malfunction	placement
refill	connection
illuminate	treatment
rebuild	

1. Choose an appliance.
2. Outline steps for repairing the appliance. Use words from the services rendered chart, manuals, diagrams, and catalogues.

Broken Appliances

Appliance Catalogues

Assembly diagrams

FIXING THE BROKEN IRON
1. Disconnect the cord.
2. Unscrew the bottom.
3. Repair the bendable coils.

by Stephanie

INTEGRATING WITH THE REAL WORLD

MADISON AVENUE AD MAKERS

skills: thinking of descriptive words containing prefixes and suffixes
using descriptive words in context

Display product charts on a large chart rack. Product charts that have been completed with word lists can be used in various writing activities: writing a jingle, slogan, letter recommending the product, or other advertisement.

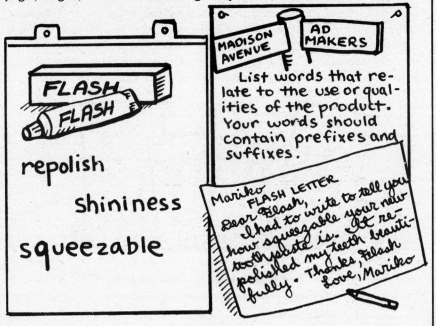

FLASH FLASH

repolish

shininess

squeezable

MADISON AVENUE   AD MAKERS

List words that relate to the use or qualities of the product. Your words should contain prefixes and suffixes.

Mariko
FLASH LETTER
Dear Flash,
I had to write to tell you how squeezable your new toothpaste is. It repolished my teeth beautifully. Thanks, Flash.
Love, Mariko

FIX IT UP

skill: identifying words that contain prefixes and suffixes
understanding the meanings of prefixes and suffixes
skimming

Collect sets of directions that describe how to make or assemble something. Have the children skim the directions to find words that contain prefixes and suffixes, and circle them. Then they rewrite the directions, replacing the circled words with synonyms or phrases that are similar in meaning but maintain the original context and continuity.

ASSESSMENT WORKSHEET

MAIN IDEA

Name _____

I. Fill in the bubble that names the letter of the topic sentence.

A B C D E
○ ○ ○ ○ ○

A There are many different kinds and locations of homes. B Some homes are small. C Some homes are big. D Some homes are near the city. E Where do you live?

II. ✔ the number that matches the topic sentence.

___ 1 ___ 2 ___ 3 ___ 4

1 The rose is a flower that is often used for corsages. 2 The chrysanthemum is a flower that is eaten. 3 Some flowers are used to make teas. 4 Flowers are used for a variety of purposes.

III. Write the letter that names the topic sentence. _____

a Cinderella was crying. b Her stepsisters were angry. c Everyone in the house was upset. d The cat was running around. e The dog was barking.

IV. Write or tell your teacher the main idea of the picture in your own words.

_____
_____
_____
_____
_____

V. Write the main idea of the story in your own words.

_____
_____
_____
_____

Mary had a dog as a pet. They played together. They watched TV together. They went everywhere together.

VI. List the key words of the paragraph below. _____

_____
_____

Names of fish often give clues to their many different shapes and colors. There are yellow-tail tunas and pink salmon. Can you guess the shapes of the pipefish and the hammerhead shark?

To the teacher:
Check the appropriate column to indicate the student's performance on these main-idea exercises.

ITEM	RESPONDED APPROPRIATELY	NEEDS PRACTICE
Locates topic sentence in context (I, II, III)		
States main idea from picture or paragraph (IV, V)		
Identifies key words (VI)		

Reproducible, page 176.
Solution, page 200.

SKILLS IN THIS SECTION INCLUDE:

- identifying key words and topic sentences
- matching main ideas to various types of written material
- identifying main idea and supporting details
- developing main ideas in various ways

Main Idea/Summarizing

GENERAL ACTIVITIES

MAIN-IDEA FINDERS

skills: identifying key words and main ideas in nonfiction material
notetaking
summarizing

Glue newspaper and magazine articles and other appropriate nonfiction material from old textbooks to pages of a pad of paper. Attach the pad to a large chart under the directions.

MAIN IDEA FINDERS

Tear off a page and do one or more of the following:

~ Underline a sentence or sentences that tell the main idea.

~ mark an X on the key words.

~ write brief notes in the margin or on the back of important things to remember.

~ write a short summary.

MAINMASTS

skills: formulating main idea
differentiating and identifying main idea and supporting details

Write story or chapter titles on an assortment of empty boxes and egg cartons. Provide supplies such as dowels, construction paper, drinking straws, and glue. Children select boxes and follow the instructions. After the main idea and supporting-details masts have been made, the boats can be decorated to symbolize the central theme of the story.

MAINMASTS

1. Choose a box.

2. Read the story named on the box.

3. Make a large sail and write the main idea on it; attach it to a large mast.

4. Write details that support the main idea on small sails, and attach to smaller masts.

5. Attach the masts to the box to make a boat.

6. Decorate your boat.

MAIN STREET WORKSHEET

skills: identifying key words
using key words to develop a main idea

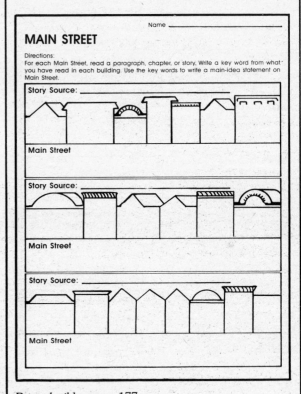

Reproducible, page 177.
Solution, page 201.

GENERAL ACTIVITIES

"MANE" IDEAS

skill: matching main ideas and key words to titles

Cut out several lion bodies and heads. Write story titles on the bodies and matching main ideas or key words on the manes.

1. Put together a lion by matching a story title with a main idea or key words.
2. Read the story to see if you are correct.

MAIN SWITCH

skill: matching titles to stories and paragraphs

On each light bulb, attach a short story or paragraph. On each switch, write a title. Attach a "wire" (string or yarn) to each of the switches. Put an answer key on back of the main switch.

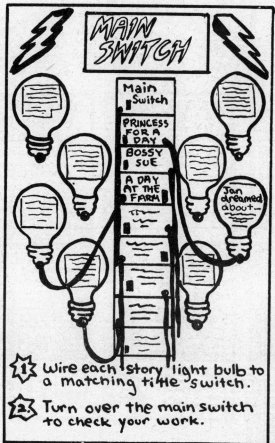

1. Wire each story light bulb to a matching title switch.
2. Turn over the main switch to check your work.

MAIN-IDEA PICTURES

skills: writing and drawing main ideas identifying main ideas of pictures

Post general categories on a bulletin board or chalkboard. Children write down an experience they have had that fits one of the categories and, on the other side of the paper, draw a picture of the experience, showing as many details as possible. The pictures are mounted under the appropriate category headings and then the other children try to guess the main ideas of their classmates' pictures. Guesses may be compared with the sentences on the backs of the pictures. Discussion of the pictures and the sentences can be useful in helping the children develop the concept of the main idea.

LEARNING CENTER

Since this center's general activities play on the word "main," the theme is continued with the title Main Entrance; a seldom-used door is the center backdrop. Or a closet door could be opened and the center housed inside.

GROUP WORK

DEVELOPING MAIN IDEAS

skills: using key words, topic sentences, and one's own thinking process to develop main ideas
comparing various ways of developing main ideas

Divide the group into three subgroups, and give copies of the same written material to each group to read. The first group lists key words from the selection and uses them to write the main idea of the selection. The second group locates the topic sentence that tells the main idea. The third group writes the main idea based on its discussion of the selection. Each subgroup then shares its main ideas, and together the whole group compares the various procedures for arriving at a main idea.

INDEPENDENT STUDY

INDEPENDENT STUDY DIAGRAMS

skills: developing main ideas from notes
following various procedures for independent study

Make, or have the children copy, diagrammatical charts such as the ones pictured. Children select one of the charts to use in independent study.

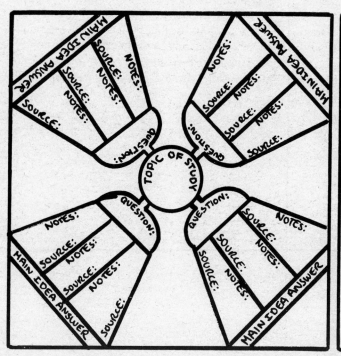

INDEPENDENT STUDY

INTEGRATING WITH THE REAL WORLD

MAIN-IDEA OUTLINE

skills: making main-idea outlines
developing main ideas from key
words and phrases

The children make outlines of phrases and key words on their independent study topics. Then they translate their outlines into complete-sentence outlines in which the main ideas follow Roman numerals and supporting ideas become the capital-letter entries.

KEY-WORD OUTLINE

FIJI *Sid*
I. Geography
 A. 300-500 islands
 B. 180th meridian
 C. Viti Levu

COMPLETE-SENTENCE OUTLINE

FIJI *Sid*
I. Many islands located just south of the equator make up the Fiji group.
 A. Depending on how you count, 300 —

TV MAIN IDEAS

skills: writing main ideas and summaries of
television programs
comparing main ideas and summaries

Children choose a television program to watch and write down its main idea in one or two sentences. Then they find the descriptive summary of the program in the TV section of the newspaper or *TV Guide,* cut it out, paste it next to the summary they have written, and compare their version with the published version.

EVERYDAY MAIN IDEAS

skill: reporting main ideas of real-life situations

On blank buttons or paper badges, write school and home situations. Each child chooses a badge to wear and observes that situation. Afterward, the children report to the group on what they have observed. During the discussion the group arrives at the main idea of each report. In time, the children may be able to give their reports in one or two main-idea sentences.

ASSESSMENT WORKSHEET

Name _____

OBSERVATION ASSESSMENT

Questions to ask the student:

1. Look at picture A for one minute. Cover the picture and tell me everything you can remember about it.
2. Look at the Ferris wheel in picture A (or the merry-go-round or some other specific part). What can you tell me about it?
3. Look at the Ferris wheel in picture B. Compare it with the Ferris wheel in picture A.
4. Look at pictures A and B and tell how they are different from each other.

Notes on student's responses:

1. Recalling visual details:

2. Observing details:

3, 4. Observing for likenesses and differences:

Reproducible, page 178.

SKILLS IN THIS SECTION INCLUDE:

- observing, describing, and comparing details
- observing change
- making inferences from data collected through observations

Observation

GENERAL ACTIVITIES

TAKE A CLOSER LOOK

skill: comparing details of objects

The activity may be done two ways:

1. Comparing specimens from different groups, such as rocks, leaves, or shells.
2. Comparing several specimens from the *same* general group.

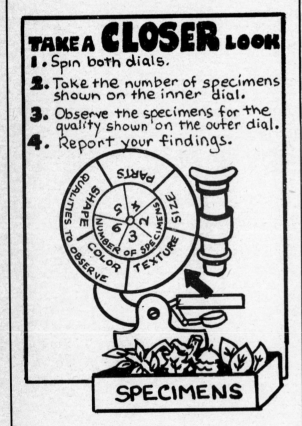

OBSERVATION OBSERVATORY

skills: observing details

On the bulletin board display magazine pictures, photographs, and study prints that fit into various categories, along with a list of questions about the objects pictured. Class discussion should explore the difficulties in gaining information only from pictures; the kinds and sizes of pictures that give the most information; and how observing the real thing compares with observing a picture of it.

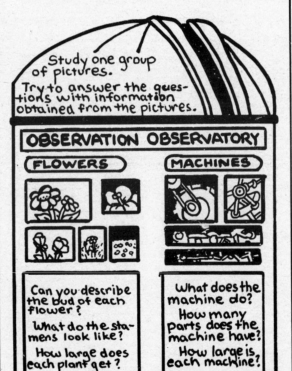

SCIENTIST'S LOG WORKSHEET

skills: seeing change
observing details
keeping a log over a period of time

SCIENTIST'S LOG

Directions:
Choose something to observe. Fill in the log as you plan and make your observations. Some of the types of things you might observe are: a tree near the school; a cocoon; the sandbox area; a bulletin board; a flowering plant; the gutter in the street in front of the school; the lunch area.

OBSERVER'S NAME: _____

ITEM OR SITUATION UNDER OBSERVATION: _____

SITE OF OBSERVATION: _____

MATERIALS USED:
RULER _____ THERMOMETER _____ MICROSCOPE _____
MAGNIFYING GLASS _____ SCALE _____ CAMERA _____
BINOCULARS _____ OTHER _____

FIRST OBSERVATION (give a complete description of item or situation): _____

DATE: _____

LATER OBSERVATIONS (note changes observed):   DATES:

Reproducible, page 179.
Solution, page 201.

GENERAL ACTIVITIES

OBSERVATION LABS

skill: categorizing by observable qualities

Make several Scientist's Laboratory folders. The "shelves" drawn on the inside may be labeled with general categories, as shown on the example at the top, or with categories specific to a particular set of specimens, such as an entomology or geology lab.

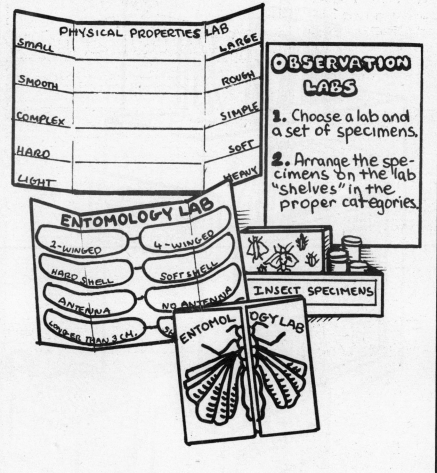

OBSERVATION SURVEYS

skills: visual memory
drawing conclusions from surveys

Set up several pairs of boxes and survey forms. One box in each pair contains objects that are alike in one way, such as color, shape, or type, while the other contains the same number of objects that are dissimilar in the same way (*different* colors, shapes, types). The child doing the survey chooses a pair of boxes and asks another child to look at the contents of the first box for thirty to sixty seconds. Then the surveyor removes the box, asks the observer to name remembered objects, and enters the number on the survey form. The process is repeated with the second box. After several children have been surveyed, the surveyor looks for patterns in the observations and writes them in the Tentative Conclusions space. The surveyor may continue to see if these conclusions hold true for many samples.

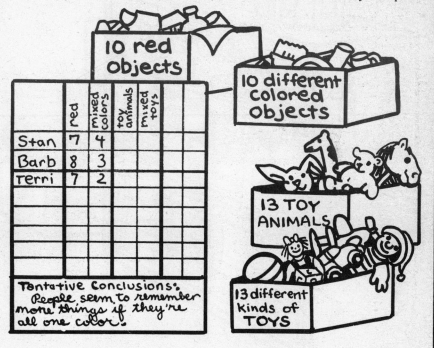

LEARNING CENTER

A bookshelf provides front, back, and side space for displaying materials, and can be arranged so that it partitions off an area of the classroom.

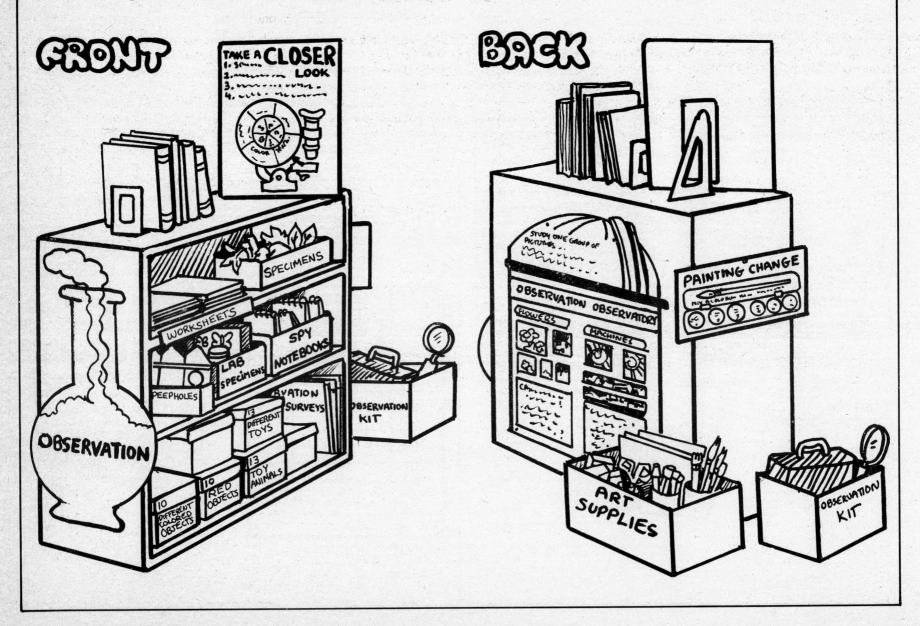

GROUP WORK

HOW DO YOU SEE IT?

skills: observing from different angles
observing details

Set an unfamiliar object, such as a jicama, a carburetor, or the inner workings of an old radio, on a table. Children place themselves at varying distances from the object, and in different positions, such as sitting and standing, and at the side of, in back of, or around the table. Children describe the object from their vantage points and discuss the similarities and differences of their observations.

SCAVENGER HUNT

skills: observing details
categorizing

Prepare a worksheet with a list of descriptions for which children find matching objects. Teams of children locate objects and tell how these objects correspond to the given descriptions.

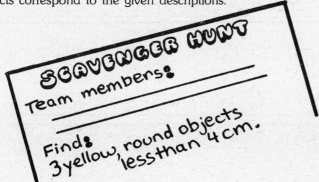

INDEPENDENT STUDY

PAINTING CHANGE

skill: observing change

Children select and perform one or more of the numbered tasks and then describe the changes that occur. Their observations can be recorded on the art paper used for the task or on a worksheet supplied by the teacher.

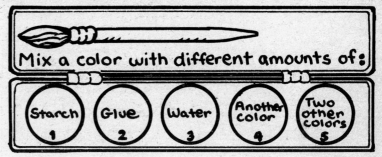

SPY NOTEBOOKS

skills: observing details
observing change

After a number of children have recorded their observations in a notebook they can discuss any patterns they see developing over a period of time.

INDEPENDENT STUDY

PEEPHOLE DRAWINGS

skills: observing details
categorizing

Make a set of task cards with different-sized holes cut out. The finished drawings are displayed so that others can guess what object was used.

INTEGRATING WITH THE REAL WORLD

OBSERVING PATTERNS

skills: observing visual and behavioral patterns
making comparisons

Children choose a pattern or routine to observe at home, and draw or write descriptions of what they see. In discussion, compare children's descriptions of similar patterns.

INTEGRATING WITH THE REAL WORLD

SENSES TAKING WORKSHEET

skills: observing with the five senses
using descriptive words

Variation:
Children fill in the worksheet for an imaginary trip, such as to the beach, amusement park, or pet store.

SENSES TAKING

Name _____

A trip to _____   In the first column, name the stops you make on your trip. In the other columns, describe what you see, hear, smell, taste, and feel at each stop.

STOPS YOU MAKE	👁	👂	👃	👄	✋

Reproducible, page 180.
Solution, page 201.

ASSESSMENT WORKSHEET

Name _____

SEEING RELATIONSHIPS

CATEGORIZING:
Put an X on the pictures that belong in the same group as a ball. These belong in the same group because

button   donut   bat

_____

net

wheel

CATEGORIZING:
Add three more pictures that belong in the group. These belong in the group because

_____

CAUSE AND EFFECT: Match each cause to its effect by drawing connecting lines.

CAUSES	EFFECTS
He put too much air in the ball.	The ball went into the stands.
The batter hit a home run.	He paid the man $50.00.
The golfer hit the ball into a window.	He had to buy a new ball.

SEQUENCE: Arrange the pictures in order by putting a number inside each picture.

BRUINS 2
TROJANS 0

OTHER RELATIONSHIPS: Teacher-designed activity to assess student's ability to understand other relationships such as time, place, and analogies.

Reproducible, page 181.
Solution, page 201.

SKILLS IN THIS SECTION INCLUDE:

- categorizing, classifying, and sequencing information
- recognizing cause-and-effect relationships

Seeing Relationships

GENERAL ACTIVITIES

JACK IN THE BOX

skills: categorizing
classifying

Fill a box with objects and pictures and prepare order forms listing various categories. Children can check their work by showing the order and objects to the teacher or by recording the order number and the objects used to fill it on a simple recording sheet.

Variation:
Children place objects on a paper plate and another child writes an order to fit the objects.

CLASSIFYING WORKSHEET

skill: classifying

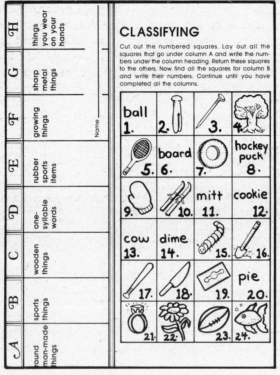

Reproducible, page 182.
Solution, page 202.

DISASTER FLICKS

skills: identifying causes and effects of historical events

List historical disasters on a chart made to resemble a movie marquee. A child chooses one of the events and does research on it, looking for causes and effects. Then the student writes and/or illustrates its causes and negative and positive effects on a roll of paper.

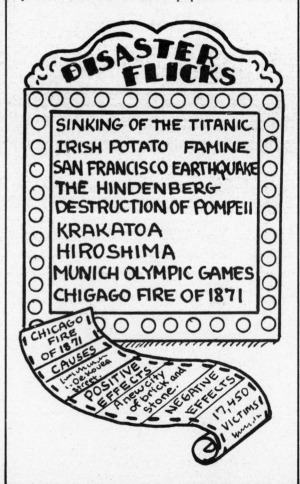

GENERAL ACTIVITIES

CAUSE-AND-EFFECT BINGO WORKSHEET

skill: matching causes and effects

If a worksheet is used as a group Bingo game, label one die with C, A, U, S, E and FREE, and one with 1, 2, 3, 4, 5 and FREE.

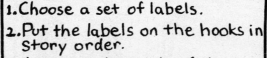

CAUSE-AND-EFFECT BINGO

To use as a worksheet for one person:
1. Find an effect to match each cause.
2. Indicate matching causes and effects with the same number. Use a new number for each pair you find.

Reproducible, page 183.
Solution, page 202.

(2 to 6 players)

To use as a Bingo game:
1. The players use a special pair of dice, and each gets a worksheet.
2. Each player in turn:
   a. Rolls the dice and locates the box on the top half of the worksheet indicated on the dice.
   b. Finds the effect on the bottom half of the worksheet that matches the cause.
   c. X's out both the cause and the effect boxes, if the group agrees with the choices.
3. The first player to complete a row across, up and down, or diagonally in either half of the worksheet is the winner.

THE T-SHIRT SHOP

skill: arranging sentences in story sequence

Make up simple stories that are three to five sentences in length. Write each sentence on a label, and color-code the labels to show which sentences go together.

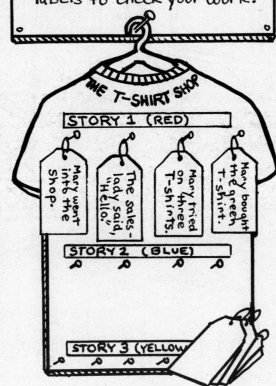

SEQUENCE GRIDS

skill: creating new sequences

Prepare a set of picture or word-sequence strips and several large cross-grid patterns. Children choose a sequence strip and copy it onto a cross grid. Then they write or draw in new sequences to fit the grid outline.

LEARNING CENTER

Cutting boards can be purchased in fabric or variety stores.
They make effective display boards and room dividers.

GROUP WORK

INDEPENDENT STUDY

STORYBOOK RINGS

skill: categorizing

Children name things from a story the group has read or is reading, and write them on wordcards. Help the children categorize the cards. Make an envelope for each category and file the corresponding wordcards within. Attach all the envelopes from one story to a chart ring that names the story or book.

CAUSE-AND-EFFECT CHARTS

skill: developing causes and effects for a given situation

Make two cause/effect charts and laminate them so that they may be used many times. Divide the group in half, and give each half a chart on which the same situation has been written. Each group fills in causes and effects on its chart. The group that lists the greatest number of reasonable causes and effects may suggest the next situation to be used.

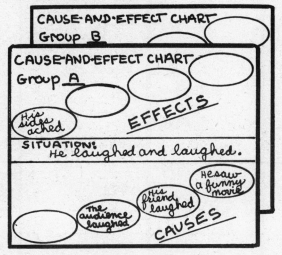

TAPED-TOGETHER STORIES

*skills: recalling important story events
        recalling story sequence*

Each child chooses an event to illustrate from a story the group has read. When the children finish their illustrations, they arrange the pictures in story sequence, tape them together, and display the story strip in the classroom.

ENCYCLOPEDIA OF CAUSE AND EFFECT

skill: researching historical events for causes and effects

Make a chart to resemble books on a shelf. Tape or staple several sheets of paper to the "spine" of each book and label the top sheet with a historical event. Each child chooses an event to research and writes its causes and effects on the extra sheets.

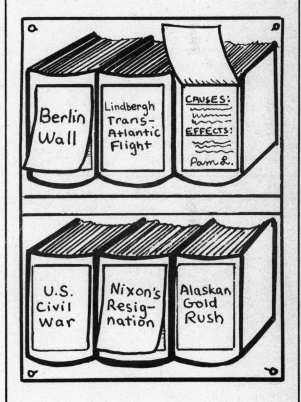

INDEPENDENT STUDY

INTEGRATING WITH THE REAL WORLD

INDEPENDENT STUDY SATELLITES

skills: categorizing subtopics within a main topic
researching

Children use cottage cheese cartons, boxes, or other containers as bases for their satellites, labeling them with their independent study topics. The children think of information categories related to their topics and label the first "arms" of their satellites with these categories. They add information to the major categories in their topic as their study progresses.

PERSONAL TIME LINES

skills: seeing time relationships
making time lines

Children make up their own personal times lines, from birth to the present. Major events in their lives are written, drawn, or illustrated with photographs from home in time sequence.

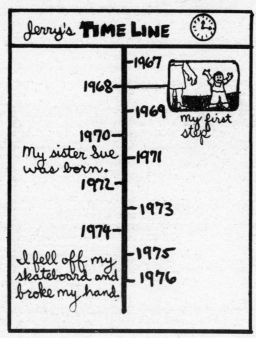

HOMEWORK CATEGORIZING

skill: categorizing

Children clean out a drawer, shelf, or cupboard at home and sort the items into several categories. Afterward, they make lists of the categories and items and bring them to school.

SEQUENCE SQUIGGLES

skill: sequencing steps in real-life procedures

Make a squiggle chart listing a variety of everyday events. Younger children might start with simple squiggles of only three or four spaces; older children may draw more complex designs.

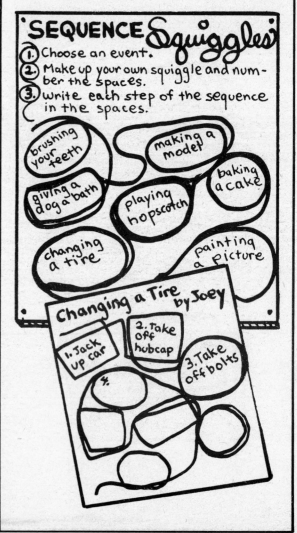

ASSESSMENT WORKSHEET

DRAWING CONCLUSIONS

		ASSIGNMENTS (for teacher use)

Check the evidence that supports the conclusion.

CONCLUSION	EVIDENCE	
The pet got out of the cage.	___ the cage was empty.	_____
	___ The pet was hiding under the newspaper in the cage.	_____
	___ Nobody could find the pet.	_____
	___ Everyone saw the pet run away.	_____

Write a conclusion for the evidence.

EVIDENCE	CONCLUSION	
People were happy.		
Cake was served.	_____	_____
Presents were opened.	_____	_____
Everyone sang.	_____	_____

Match each conclusion with evidence.

CONCLUSION	EVIDENCE	
Mickey Mouse is Donald Duck's friend.	His picture is in the Hall of Fame and watches have his picture on them.	_____
Mickey Mouse is famous.	He is drawn by someone and doesn't really talk.	_____
Mickey Mouse is a cartoon character.	He is shown holding hands with him and they play together.	_____

Reproducible, page 184.
Solution, page 202.

SKILLS IN THIS SECTION INCLUDE:

- identifying and developing evidence to support a conclusion
- developing conclusions related to given evidence

Drawing Conclusions

GENERAL ACTIVITIES

CONCLUSION CONNECTORS

skills: creating causes and effects
seeing causes and effects as evidence and conclusions

Prepare a set of connector strips and staple blank pads of paper onto the strips where the sentence is incomplete. Children read the strips and add either the evidence or the conclusion that would complete the statements.

CHARACTER CONCLUSIONS WORKSHEET

skill: locating evidence to support a conclusion

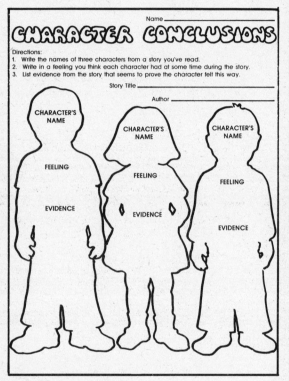

Reproducible, page 185.
Solution, page 202.

HOPPING TO CONCLUSIONS WORKSHEET

skill: identifying evidence to support a conclusion

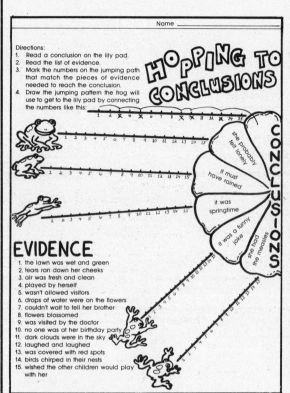

Reproducible, page 186.
Solution, page 203.

GENERAL ACTIVITIES

LEGAL BRIEFS

skills: selecting evidence to support a conclusion
developing evidence needed to support a conclusion

Develop a set of legal briefs by writing a charge and a list of related and unrelated evidence on the inside of a manila folder. Children select and read a brief and fill out an evidence form made by the teacher for the case. Some evidence can come from the list inside the brief; other evidence may be reasoned by the child. Additional legal briefs can be created by the children for their classmates to use.

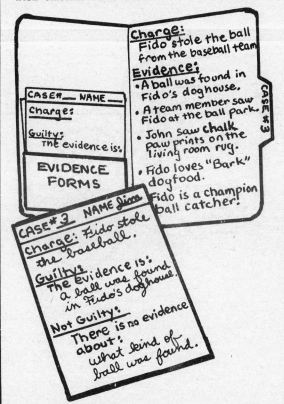

Charge:
Fido stole the ball from the baseball team

Evidence:
• A ball was found in Fido's doghouse.
• A team member saw Fido at the ball park.
• John saw chalk paw prints on the living room rug.
• Fido loves "Bark" dogfood.
• Fido is a champion ball catcher!

CASE #___ NAME ___
Charge:
Guilty:
  The evidence is:

EVIDENCE FORMS

CASE #3　NAME Lissa
charge: Fido stole the baseball.
Guilty:
The evidence is:
a ball was found in Fido's doghouse.
Not Guilty:
There is no evidence about:
what kind of ball was found.

DON'T JUMP TO CONCLUSIONS

skills: developing evidence to support a given conclusion
developing conclusions related to given evidence

Make the gameboard and kangaroo pieces out of heavy cardboard. The players need to listen to each other's evidence in order to verify, negate, or question its relationship to the conclusion.

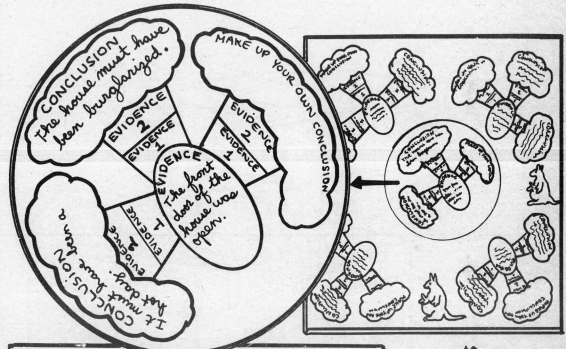

CONCLUSION
The house must have been burglarized.

MAKE UP YOUR OWN CONCLUSION

EVIDENCE 2
EVIDENCE 1
EVIDENCE 2
EVIDENCE 1
EVIDENCE
The front door of the house was open.

CONCLUSION
It must have been a dog toy.

EVIDENCE

DIRECTIONS:　　　2 to 4 players

1. "Hop" a kangaroo to a grove of trees.

2. Read the evidence in the circle at the base of the trees.

3. Move to one of the two conclusions, or make up one.

4. Give (orally) two more pieces of evidence that would support the conclusion selected.

LEARNING CENTER

Housing all materials in a large box provides a learning center that is compact, movable, and easy to store. This is especially useful for teachers who share rooms, have small classrooms, team teach, or move between classrooms or schools during the day.

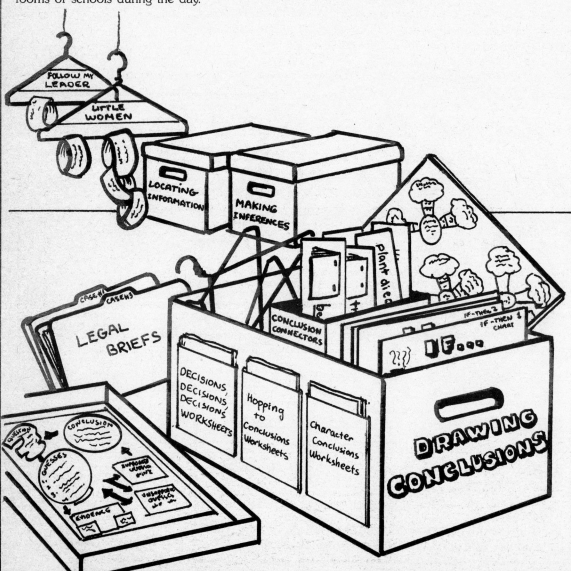

GROUP WORK

WHO STOLE THE COOKIES FROM THE COOKIE JAR?

skill: developing evidence to support a conclusion

Use a real cookie jar or decorate a coffee can to resemble a cookie jar. Cut out paper cookies and label each one with the name of a child in the class, a story character, or a famous person. Draw one to four chocolate chips on each cookie. One child takes a cookie from the jar and, without showing it to the others, gives the same number of clues (evidence) as there are chocolate chips. The others try to conclude from the clues whose name is on the cookie.

GROUP WORK

CHART TALK

*skills: locating evidence to support tentative conclusions
researching*

Outline the flow chart on cardboard and laminate so it can be reused. Write in a question and have children respond with guesses before doing research. After collecting data, children write down any evidence that relates to the question and attach it to the chart. The original guesses are re-evaluated in terms of the evidence. Guesses that are not supported by the evidence are rejected; those that are supported by evidence are incorporated into a conclusion that answers the question.

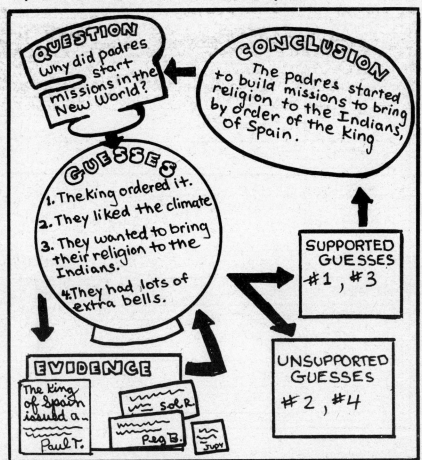

INDEPENDENT STUDY

IF/THEN CHART

skill: applying conclusions to a new situation

Make several IF/THEN charts. The children may devise their own way to demonstrate the "IFs" or they may be directed to science books or other sources for suggestions on demonstrations.

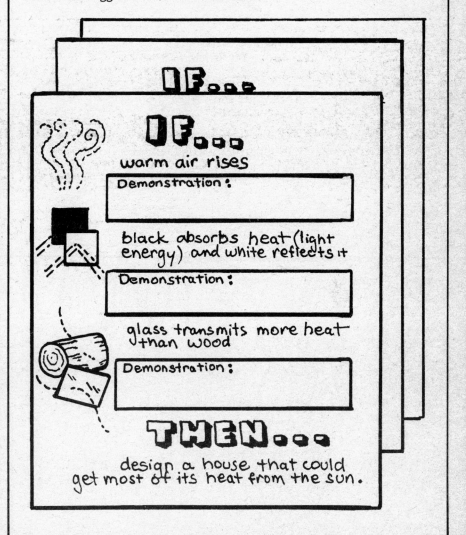

INDEPENDENT STUDY

CONCLUSION CHAINS

skill: locating evidence to support a conclusion

1. Choose a hanger and read the book named.
2. Read the conclusion links.
3. Find evidence in the story to support each conclusion.
4. Write each piece of evidence on a link and attach to the proper conclusion.

LITTLE WOMEN

THE HUNDRED DRESSES

CONCLUSION Wanda was not a good reader.

CONCLUSION Wanda was poor.

CONCLUSION Wanda was unhappy.

CONCLUSION

CONCLUSION

EVIDENCE She wore the same dress everyday.

EVIDENCE She lived in a poor neighborhood.

INTEGRATING WITH THE REAL WORLD

DECISIONS, DECISIONS, DECISIONS WORKSHEET

skill: identifying evidence used in making decisions

Children complete their worksheets at home. In the classroom, ask them to describe how decisions are made in their families.

Name _____

DECISIONS, DECISIONS, DECISIONS

Directions:
1. Write in three of your family's decisions.
2. For each decision, tell how family members did — or did not — support the decision.

DECISION

Family Member	Supporting/Not Supporting the Decision

DECISION

Family Member	Supporting/Not Supporting the Decision

DECISION

Family Member	Supporting/Not Supporting the Decision

Reproducible, page 187.
Solution, page 203.

2

RELEVANT REINFORCERS FOR THE BASIC SKILLS

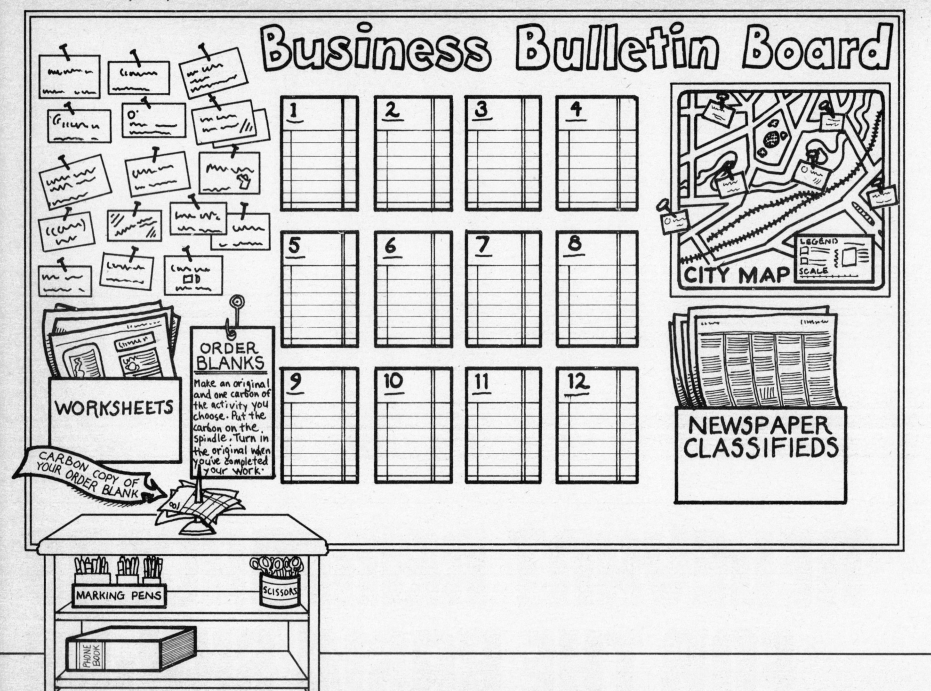

The process of obtaining business cards, as well as the use of business cards with a specific task, can be a learning experience. Concepts related to career exploration can be reinforced by having the children interview or write businessmen and women requesting career information and samples of business cards.

Although the activities using business cards represent skills from various subject areas, the teacher can choose to display those activities that focus on one particular skill, such as alphabetizing, or one subject area, such as language arts.

The tasks are written on sales slips, and the children fill in the number and description of their task on two copies of an order blank. One copy is filed with the teacher as a record, or "contract," of the work to be done. The second copy is kept by the child and attached to the completed work when it is submitted to the teacher for review or correcting.

Business Cards

1.

Choose twenty or thirty business cards.

Put the cards in alphabetical order, using either the name of the business, the name of the person, or the name of the street or city where the business is located.

2.

Choose twenty business cards.

Group the cards by size, color, shape, type of business, etc.

Make a label to show how you grouped the cards.

William Morris, D.D.S.

Medical People

Janet Green, M.D.

Allison Grant
Dental Hygienist

3.

Use the dictionary to look up words on the business cards that could be replaced by synonyms.

Rewrite the cards using the synonyms you find.

Example: Tom's Tiny Eatery
Tom's Small Restaurant

4.

Choose ten business cards.

Read the address on each of the cards.

Put the cards in numerical order, using the addresses.

5.

Choose six business cards that have abbreviations printed on them.

Write out the words that are abbreviated.

Write abbreviations for words that could be abbreviated but are not.

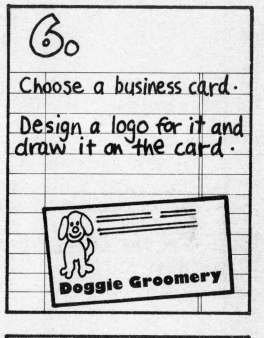

Mister
Mr. James T. Wynn
Carpenter

360 S. 5th St. South Fifth
L.A., California Los Angeles, Ca.

6.

Choose a business card.

Design a logo for it and draw it on the card.

Doggie Groomery

7.

Select a newspaper classified page.

Read the want ads on the page.

Match some of the business cards that could provide the services needed by those who placed the ads.

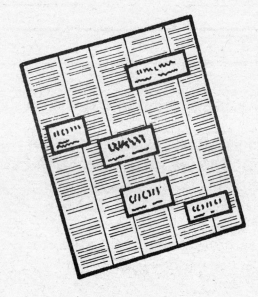

8.

Choose a business card for a career you would like to have.

Research the career by reading books and interviewing someone who is in that field.

Write some of the things you learn on the back of the card or on another piece of paper.

9.

Choose several business cards.

Look at a city map and match the addresses on the cards to the correct streets on the map.

Pin the cards up on the map.

10.

Choose a business card.

Write a list of questions to ask the owner about his business.

Call or write the business to get the answers to your questions.

11.

Choose a business card.

Make up a rhyme or slogan for the person or the business.

Write it on the card.

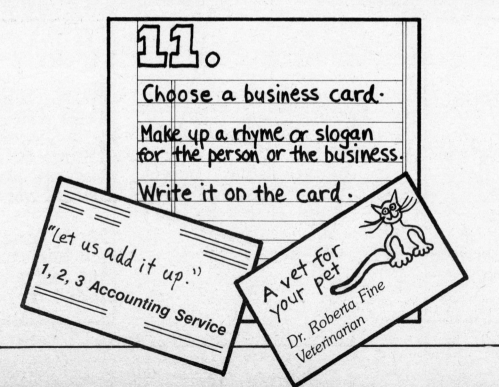

"Let us add it up."

1, 2, 3 Accounting Service

A vet for your pet

Dr. Roberta Fine
Veterinarian

12.

Take a business card worksheet.

Design business cards for several of your own businesses (or pasttimes) or businesses you would like to have.

13.

Take a business card worksheet.

Make cards for your friends and classmates, describing talents and skills they have.

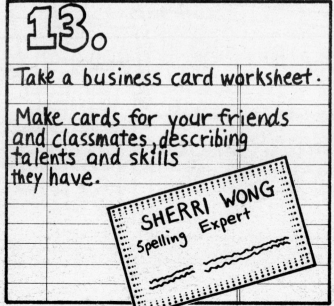

Name _____

BUSINESS CARD WORKSHEET

Check ✔ the activities you will do.
___ Design business cards for several of your own businesses (or pastimes).
___ Design cards for businesses or jobs you would like to have.
___ Design cards for friends and classmates describing talents and skills they have.

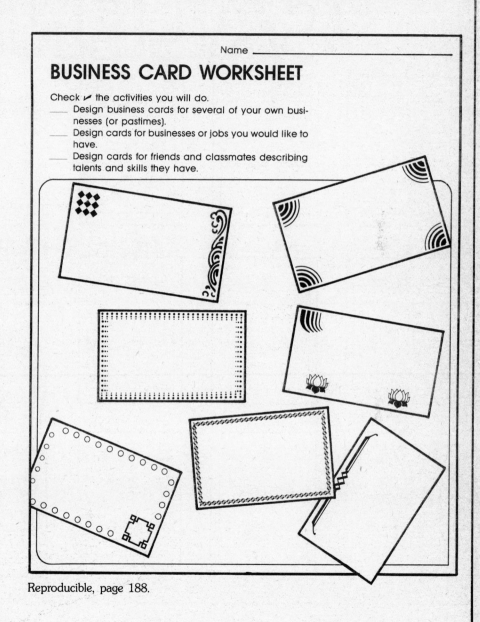

Reproducible, page 188.

CALENDARS

Do all the tasks from this calendar on your own calendar page.

SUNDAY	MONDAY	TUESDAY	WEDNESDAY	THURSDAY	FRIDAY	SATURDAY
	Draw ten green dots on the third day of the month. **1**	Put an X on the first Monday of the month. **2**	Circle each date of the second week in the month. **3**	Draw a picture of yourself on your favorite day of the fourth week of the month. **4**	Paint the name of the date for the twenty-first day of the month. **5**	Write the abbreviations for the date of the thirtieth day of the month. **6**
Draw a sun or cloud to show the weather for the second day of any week. **7**	Color in red the date you think is the worst day in the first week of the month. **8**	Put a line under each numeral of the fourth week of the month. **9**	Put a different letter of the alphabet on each even-numbered date in the month. **10**	Write the birthdate and name of any person in the square that has the same number of his or her birthday. **11**	Replace the numeral of the date that is the same as your age with a Roman numeral. **12**	List the first, second, third, and fourth things you did when you woke up this morning on the third Monday of the month. **13**
Write your initials on the date of the second-to-last day of the month. **14**	Mark the first day of the month with a blue square. **15**	Draw a triangle on any Saturday or Wednesday that has an old-numbered date. **16**	Write your name, last name first, in any square. **17**	Jot a note to yourself on the second Friday of the month. **18**	Write your telephone number in the square that is the same as the first digit in your phone number. **19**	Draw a tooth in the square that tells how many teeth you have. **20**
Play tic-tac-toe in the square for the third Thursday of the month. **21**	Print in capital letters the name of the day for the seventh day of the second week. **22**	Trace with a green crayon over the numeral of the date that follows the seventeenth. **23**	Draw a black cat on your unlucky number. **24**	Redesign one of the squares to look like the inside of a box. **25**	Write in more numerals next to the numeral in any Tuesday to make a larger number. **26**	Write the first letter of the day in the square of the eighteenth of the month. **27**
Draw seven ants going over a hill in any square you like! **28**	Write your teacher's name in the square that tells the age you think he or she is. **29**	Fill in an empty square with its date written in mirror writing. **30**	Outline in purple the square of the fifth day of the fourth week. **31**			

CALENDAR PAGES FOR YOU TO USE

CALENDAR STRIPS

Calendar pages are an alternative to using worksheets. They provide the children with a new medium on which to practice math skills, and for teachers are a ready-made resource to use in math followup or supplementary activities. Old calendars can be obtained from printers, stationery stores, businesses, or the children's homes.

The tasks can be coded for difficulty or placed in sequential order to correspond with texts and other math materials used in the classroom. Descriptions of the tasks to be done with the calendar pages are written on datebook pages or other small calendar pages, such as those from desk calendars.

Calendars

Note: Activities on this page are generally easier than those on the following pages.

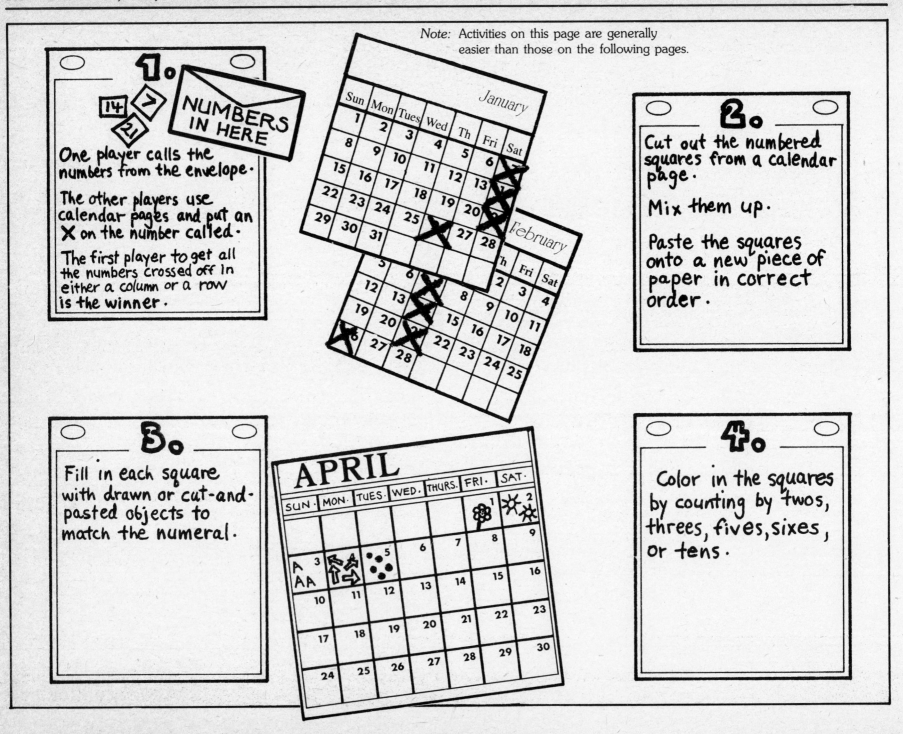

1.

One player calls the numbers from the envelope.

The other players use calendar pages and put an X on the number called.

The first player to get all the numbers crossed off in either a column or a row is the winner.

2.

Cut out the numbered squares from a calendar page.

Mix them up.

Paste the squares onto a new piece of paper in correct order.

3.

Fill in each square with drawn or cut-and-pasted objects to match the numeral.

4.

Color in the squares by counting by twos, threes, fives, sixes, or tens.

Note: Activities on this page are of "medium" difficulty, compared with the others in this section.

5.

Add the numbers in each row.

Add the numbers in each column.

Add the numbers in the diagonals.

Add the numbers in every other square.

Add the even numbers.

Add the odd numbers.

Toss three beans or peanuts onto the page and add the numbers they land on.

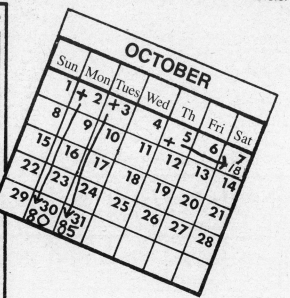

6.

Fill in each square with the number words for the numeral.

Use cardinal (one, two, etc.) or ordinal (first, second, etc.) words.

7.

Write a date in each square.

Use words, numerals, and abbreviations to write the dates in different ways.

Note: Activities on these pages are generally more difficult than those on the preceding pages.

8.

Make up equations using +, −, and ✗.

Use all the numbers on the strip.

Think about using negative and positive numbers.

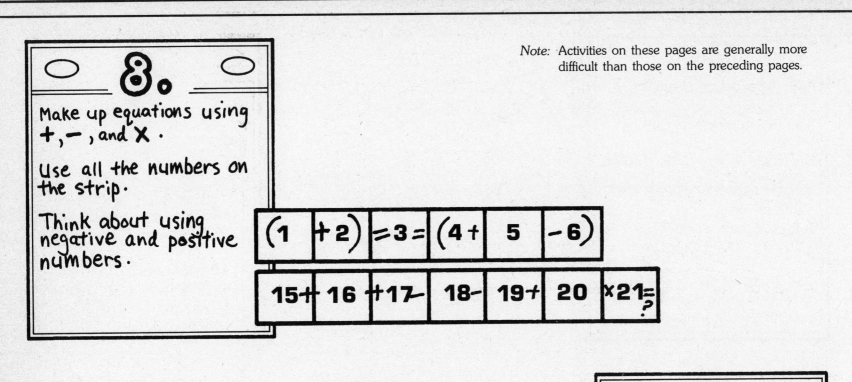

(1 | + 2) | = 3 = | (4 + | 5 | − 6)

15+ | 16 | +17− | 18− | 19+ | 20 | ✗21= ?

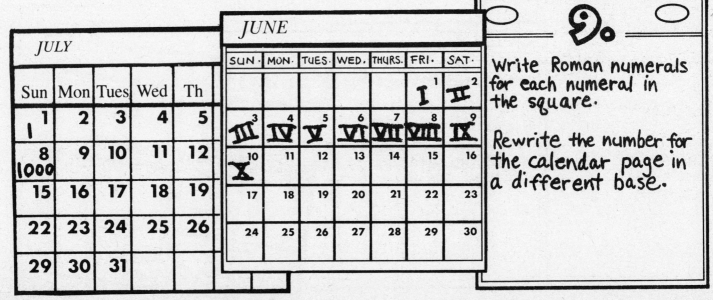

9.

Write Roman numerals for each numeral in the square.

Rewrite the number for the calendar page in a different base.

SEPTEMBER

SUN.	MON.	TUES.	WED.	THURS.	FRI.	SAT.
					1	2
3	4	5	6	7	8	9
10	11	12	13	14	15	16
17	18	19	20	21	22	23
24	25	26	27	28	29	30

10.

Write fraction statements to go with the calendar page.

Color in the spaces to prove your statements.

4/30 = 2/15 of September are Thursdays.

5/30 = 1/6 of September are Fridays

11.

Rewrite all the numerals in a row in order so that each follows the other.

Put commas in to make one numeral.

Read the numeral to a friend.

Write the number words for the numeral.

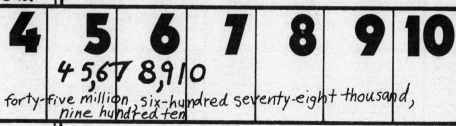

4 5,67 8,910

forty-five million, six-hundred seventy-eight thousand, nine hundred ten

SUNDAY	MONDAY	TUESDAY	WEDNESDAY
	1 Draw ten green dots on the third day of the month.	**2** Put an X on the first Monday of the month.	**3** Circle each date of the second week in the month.
7 Draw a sun or cloud to show the weather for the second day of any week.	**8** Color in red the date you think is the worst day in the first week of the month.	**9** Put a line under each numeral of the fourth week of the month.	**10** Put a different letter of the alphabet on each even-numbered date in the month.
14 Write your initials on the date of the second-to-last day of the month.	**15** Mark the first day of the month with a blue square.	**16** Draw a triangle on any Saturday or Wednesday that has an odd-numbered date.	**17** Write your name, last name first, in any square.
21 Play tic-tac-toe in the square for the third Thursday of the month.	**22** Print in capital letters the name of the day for the seventh day of the second week.	**23** Trace with a green crayon over the numeral of the date that follows the seventeenth.	**24** Draw a black cat on your unlucky number.
28 Draw seven ants going over a hill in any square you like!	**29** Write your teacher's name in the square that tells the age you think he or she is.	**30** Fill in an empty square with its date written in mirror writing.	**31** Outline in purple the square of the fifth day of the fourth week.

THURSDAY	FRIDAY	SATURDAY
4 Draw a picture of yourself on your favorite day of the fourth week of the month.	**5** Paint the name of the date for the twenty-first day of the month.	**6** Write the abbreviations for the date of the thirtieth day of the month.
11 Write the birthdate and name of any person in the square that has the same number of his or her birthday.	**12** Replace the numeral of the date that is the same as your age with a Roman numeral.	**13** List the first, second, third, and fourth things you did when you woke up this morning on the third Monday of the month.
18 Jot a note to yourself on the second Friday of the month.	**19** Write your telephone number in the square that is the same as the first digit in your phone number.	**20** Draw a tooth in the square that tells how many teeth you have.
25 Redesign one of the squares to look like the inside of a box.	**26** Write in more numerals next to the numeral in any Tuesday to make a larger number.	**27** Write the first letter of the day in the square of the eighteenth of the month.

12 Do all the tasks from this calendar on your own calendar page.

This set of activities uses coloring books in a new way—as a means of reinforcing basic skills the children are learning—and do not promote the traditional use of coloring books. Using coloring books is an especially effective technique, because they are familiar to, and liked by, most children. The books can either be purchased or brought from home by the children.

Any activity can be applied to any coloring book page the teacher chooses, or the children can select their own coloring-book pages to work on.

Other ways of using coloring books include:

- Having the children use their own coloring book as a workbook for all the activities.
- Stapling together sets of coloring-book pages for children to use with each activity.
- Attaching a letter to a coloring book outlining various activities to be done with coloring-book pages at home.

Coloring Books

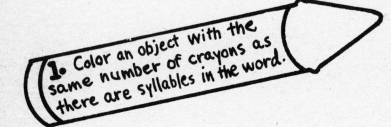

1. Color an object with the same number of crayons as there are syllables in the word.

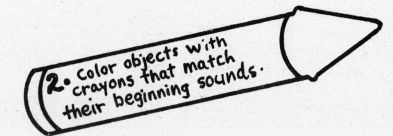

2. Color objects with crayons that match their beginning sounds.

3. Label objects with color words for a friend to read and color.

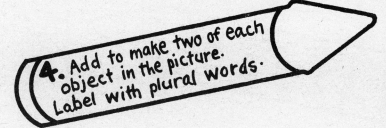

4. Add to make two of each object in the picture. Label with plural words.

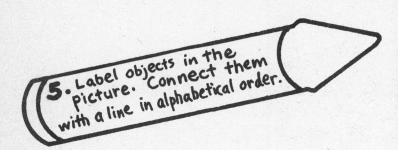

5. Label objects in the picture. Connect them with a line in alphabetical order.

6. Label Objects. Add color adjectives and color them with those colors.

7. Add words and objects to make a poster, advertisement, or sign.

SWIM, SAIL, RELAX in HAWAII

8. Fill in an object's shape with its name or with adjectives for it.

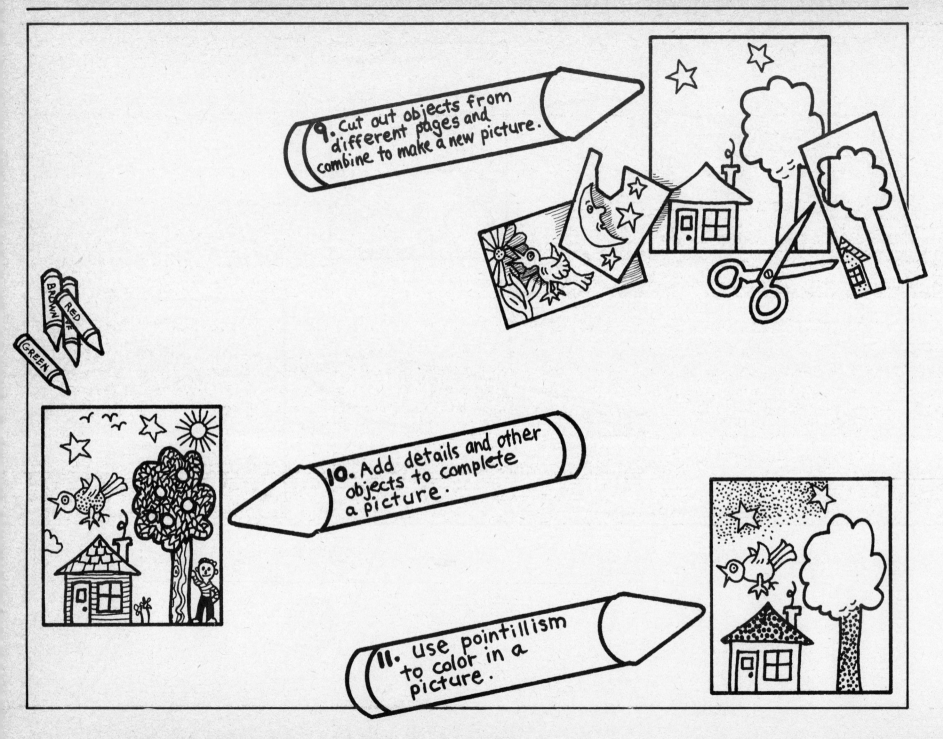

9. Cut out objects from different pages and combine to make a new picture.

10. Add details and other objects to complete a picture.

11. Use pointillism to color in a picture.

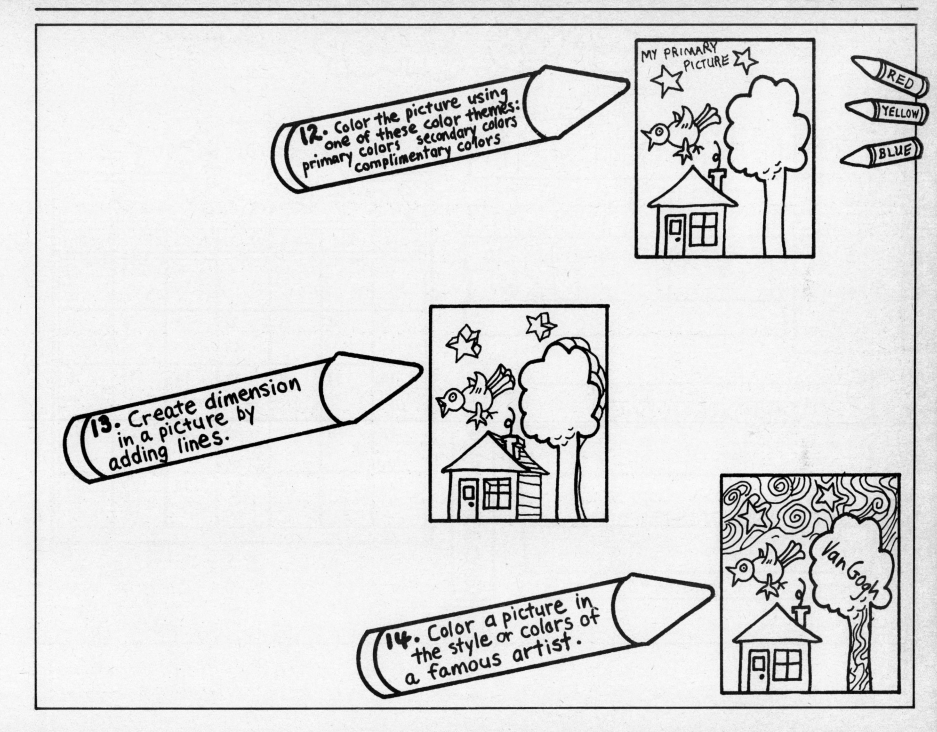

12. Color the picture using one of these color themes: primary colors, secondary colors, complimentary colors

MY PRIMARY PICTURE

RED
YELLOW
BLUE

13. Create dimension in a picture by adding lines.

14. Color a picture in the style or colors of a famous artist.

Van Gogh

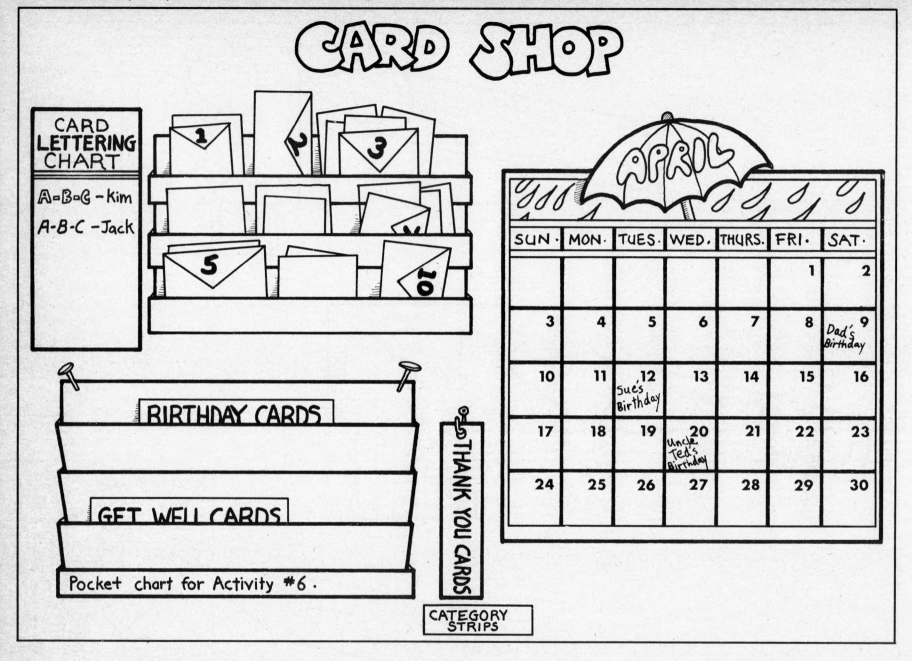

A collection of new and used greeting cards for various occasions and suggested activities provides children with opportunities to apply learned skills to familiar materials. The message, occasion, price, design, and stock number on a greeting card can become the basis for language-arts and math-oriented activities. The tasks suggested can be used with almost any greeting card, and are not dependent on a card for a particular occasion.

Task cards are made by writing descriptions of the activities on envelopes. The children select a task and do their work on the greeting cards stored behind the "task envelopes."

Greeting Cards

④ Choose six cards. Arrange them in numerical order according to one of the numerals on the backs.

Hallmark 324

Charm Craft 25

Bonanza 896

American Card Co. 6308

Buzza 7133

⑤ Choose five cards. Write the month of the holiday on each one. Arrange them in order by month, from the beginning of the year to the end.

HAPPY VALENTINE — February

HAPPY EASTER — April

For You Mom... — May

HAPPY FISHING DAD — JUNE

MERRY CHRISTMAS — DECEMBER

⑥ Choose a category strip. Find cards to fit the category and put them in the pocket chart.

Choose twenty or more cards. Choose related or un-related category strips or write your own. Sort the cards in the categories, using the pocket chart.

- CARDS FOR FAMILY
- SENTIMENTAL CARDS
- Cards for Business Acquaintances
- GET WELL CARDS
- WEDDING CARDS
- Cards for Women
- CARDS FOR FRIENDS
- HUMOROUS CARDS
- Cards for Men
- Birthday Cards
- CONGRATULATIONS CARDS
- SEXIST CARDS

⑦ Compute the area of the front of a card in square inches or square centimeters. Compute the area for the same card, opened up. Unfold the card completely and compute that area.

24 sq.cm.

48 Sq. Cm.

Happy Birthday!

96 Square Centimeters

⑧ Add samples of lettering from greeting cards to the lettering chart.

⑨ Choose several cards. Tell who would enjoy receiving each one and why that person would like the card. Think of family, friends, famous people, and story characters.

Just for you, DAD!

This would be a good card for Papa Bear because he had nothing to eat after Goldilocks ate his porridge.

10 Fill in the greeting card inventory worksheet.

Name _____

GREETING CARD INVENTORY

Directions:
Take twenty to fifty greeting cards. Choose a category from the list below or make up your own. Sort the cards to fit the category and record the results on the graph.

CATEGORIES: Kinds of occasions (birthday, Halloween, Valentine's Day, Christmas, Hanukah, etc.); kinds of designs (flowers, abstract, cartoon, etc.); main colors used; sizes; prices; lettering style; names or types of people to receive the cards.

CATEGORY:						
1						
2						
3						
4						
5						
6						
7						
8						
9						
10						

Reproducible, page 189.

11 Think of people you would like to send greeting cards to. Initial your entries on the big calendar. Make or choose cards to send to these people. Address and mail your cards a few days early.

To the teacher:

This activity uses real-life situations to encourage consideration for others while providing practice in addressing envelopes and using a calendar as a reminder list. The activity can be a monthly or yearly one. A big calendar page for each new month can be started in the last week of the preceding month, or a master calendar for the entire year may be started, and updated as the year progresses.

APRIL

SUN.	MON.	TUES.	WED.	THURS.	FRI.	SAT.
					1	2
3	4	5	6	7	8	9 Dad's Birthday
10	11	12 Sues Birthday	13	14	15	16
17	18	19	20	21	22	23
24	25	26	27	28	29	30

Although these map activities reinforce basic skills related to a variety of subject areas, a set of tasks can be developed to help the children acquire specific map skills. The activities are numbered so that the teacher or child can relate the work to the skill required by the task.

Maps for these activities can be obtained from gas stations, travel agencies, chambers of commerce, and state or national tourist departments. In addition, the children can bring maps from home or they can be purchased from used-book stores or cut out of obsolete atlases or other books. If it is difficult to obtain a large enough supply of maps so that the children can do their work directly on the maps, these alternatives might be considered:

- Make many copies of several page-size maps.
- Try to obtain at least one map for each child so that several activities can be done on the same map.
- Adapt activities so that the children can use the same maps and do their work on separate paper.

The tasks may be written on "tour cards" and displayed in airline ticket folders obtained from airline offices or travel agencies.

Maps

TOUR 1

Plan an A-Z route with stops at places that begin with every letter of the alphabet. List each stop (your itinerary) in alphabetical order.

A-Z TRIP

Anchorage
Birchwood
Clam Gulch
Douglas
Eek
Fairbanks

TOUR 2

Choose five maps that have a scale of miles or kilometers. Arrange the maps in numerical order according to their scales.

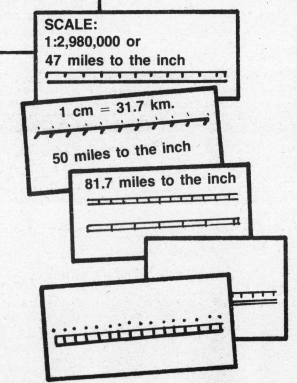

SCALE:
1:2,980,000 or
47 miles to the inch

1 cm = 31.7 km.

50 miles to the inch

81.7 miles to the inch

TOUR 3

Find several places on a map. Make up bumper-sticker rhymes to attract visitors to these places.

HAVE A WEDDING IN REDDING

ATTEND THE FAIRE IN BIG BEAR

TOUR 4

Plan a syllable trip. Starting at a one-syllable city, draw lines to show your route from one-syllable to two-syllable to three-syllable (etc.) cities.

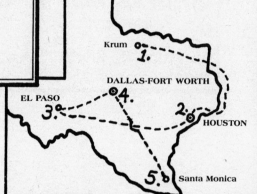

Krum

DALLAS-FORT WORTH

EL PASO

HOUSTON

Santa Monica

TOUR 5

Choose five mountain elevations. Write the elevations in numerals and number words.

SLIP MOUNTAIN MONTANA 7,290
seven thousand two hundred ninety

MT. RAINIER WASHINGTON 14,410
fourteen thousand four hundred ten

TOUR 6

Write place names in groups to show the language used to name the places.

SPANISH	FRENCH	INDIAN
Los Angeles	Baton Rouge	Anoka
San Jose	Eau Claire	Sioux City
Santa Rosa		

TOUR 7

Write five names of places you don't know how to pronounce. Use the dictionary or encyclopedia and write diacritical marks over the words to show how to say them.

RIJSWIJK,
   Netherlands
RĪS′ VĪK

GUANAJUATO,
   Mexico
GWÄ′ NÄ HWÄ′ TŌ

TOUR 8

Write six place names that use abbreviations. Now write the words the abbreviations stand for.

N. KINGSTON, RHODE ISLAND
North

SCITUATE RES., RHODE ISLAND
   Reservoir

W. WARWICK, RHODE ISLAND
West

TOUR 9

Follow the yellow brick road. Place the bricks from your home city to a place you would like to visit. Count the bricks you used. Now do the same thing with another place you would like to visit. Which place is closest to your home? If each brick represented 100 kilometers, what would the distances be?

SOUTHERN CALIFORNIA

● **Idyllwild**

8 bricks

● **Borrego Springs**

9 bricks

PACIFIC OCEAN

● **Cardiff-by-the-Sea**

TOUR 10

Connect places on your map to form geometric shapes— triangles, squares, circles, hexagons, parallelograms, trapezoids.

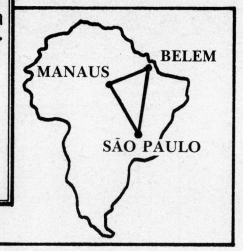

MANAUS

BELEM

SÃO PAULO

TOUR 11

Choose five capital cities. Add up the numbers of the highways that lead to each city. Which city is represented by the greatest sum?

WASHINGTON, D.C. U.S.A.

$$
\begin{array}{r}
270 \\
123 \\
95 \\
355 \\
\hline
843
\end{array}
$$

TOUR 12

Wrap up a box in a map. Compare the number of cities, towns, rivers, mountains, highways, and other features that appear on each side of the box.

12 Cities
2 Rivers
9 Mountains

WORD BAGS

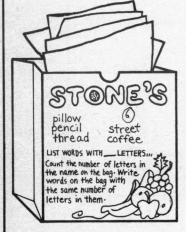

STONE'S

pillow ⑥
pencil   street
thread   coffee

LIST WORDS WITH ___ LETTERS....
Count the number of letters in the name on the bag. Write words on the bag with the same number of letters in them.

STONE'S

A L T Y   A N   B L O N G   U T Y   D I B L E   N A C K

What am I ? (Peanut)

WRITE A RIDDLE....
Use each letter of the name on the bag to begin a word that describes something you would buy at the store. Ask friends to solve the riddle.

STONE'S

O A P   O W E L S   A T M E A L   U T S   G G S   O U P

LIST ITEMS THE STORE SELLS....
Use each letter of the name on the bag as the beginning letter for an item.

STONE'S

T O P   O D A Y   P E N   I G H T S   X T R A   A V I N G S

CREATE A SLOGAN....
Use, in order, each letter of the name on the bag as the beginning letter of a word in the slogan.

STONE'S

FILL UP THE BAG....
Write names of things that could be carried in the bag. Put these words inside the bag.

STONE'S

DIRECTIONAL WORDS....
List words, phrases, and sentences that mean "front" on the front of the bag. Repeat this with the back, outside, inside, and side.

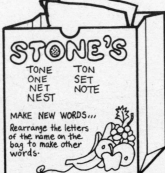

STONE'S

TONE   TON
ONE   SET
NET   NOTE
NEST

MAKE NEW WORDS....
Rearrange the letters of the name on the bag to make other words.

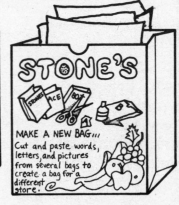

STONE'S

MAKE A NEW BAG....
Cut and paste words, letters, and pictures from several bags to create a bag for a different store.

ENTER

THE BROWN BAG RECYCLING CONTEST

carry as a purse
—Carol

take as a suitcase
—Paul

wear as shoes
— Lynn

Halloween masks
—Sam

puppets
—Tina

The words (store names) on shopping bags are used as the basis for activities that reinforce such skills such as spelling and vocabulary development. Paper or plastic shopping bags can be obtained at supermarkets or other stores, or they can be brought from home by the children.

The activities in this section have been designed to be done with bags that do not have any printing on them other than the store name. If the bags in your collection do have slogans or phrases in addition to the store name, you may have to print the store name on the other side of the bags.

Task directions can be written on the bags; completed work and materials can be stored in them.

Shopping Bags

① STONE'S

pillow   ⑥
pencil   street
thread   coffee

LIST WORDS WITH ___ LETTERS...
Count the number of letters in the name on the bag. Write words on the bag with the same number of letters in them.

② STONE'S

ALTY AN BLONG UTY DIBLE NACK

What am I ? (Peanut)

WRITE A RIDDLE...
Use each letter of the name on the bag to begin a word that describes something you would buy at the store. Ask friends to solve the riddle.

③ STONE'S

ZIPPER THREAD
STITCH 'N SEW
PAPER CUPS
PLAZA STATIONERY

FILL UP THE BAG...
Write names of things that could be carried in the bag. Put these words inside the bag.

④ STONE'S

STONE'S
Before
Ahead of

STONE'S
beside
next to

DIRECTIONAL WORDS...
List words, phrases, and sentences that mean "front" on the front of the bag. Repeat this with the back, outside, inside, and side.

⑤ STONE'S

OAP
OWELS
ATMEAL
UTS
GGS
OUP

LIST ITEMS THE STORE SELLS...

Use each letter of the name on the bag as the beginning letter for an item.

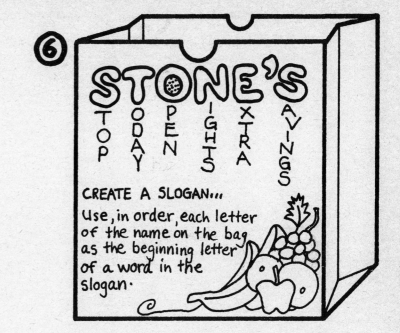

⑥ STONE'S

TOP
ODAY
PEN
IGHTS
XTRA
AVINGS

CREATE A SLOGAN...

Use, in order, each letter of the name on the bag as the beginning letter of a word in the slogan.

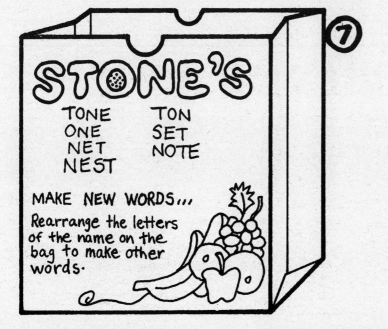

⑦ STONE'S

TONE   TON
ONE   SET
NET   NOTE
NEST

MAKE NEW WORDS...

Rearrange the letters of the name on the bag to make other words.

⑧ STONE'S

MAKE A NEW BAG...

Cut and paste words, letters, and pictures from several bags to create a bag for a different store.

3

WORKSHEETS

FOLLOWING DIRECTIONS

1. Write your name in the upper right-hand corner. Circle the first and last letter. Write the date under your name.

2. Write your name on the line in the lower left-hand corner.

3. Write your first initial and your last name above the box in the upper left-hand corner.

4. Write your initials in the circle. Underline your last initial.

5. Write your name in capital letters in the boxes in the lower right-hand corner. Use one box for each letter. Color in any empty boxes.

6. Write your last name down the left-hand side and your first name down the right-hand side of the paper. Number each letter in your name.

7. Write your last name to the right of the X. Cross out every other letter.

Teacher option: Have student follow oral directions to
_____   complete a task
_____   go to a location

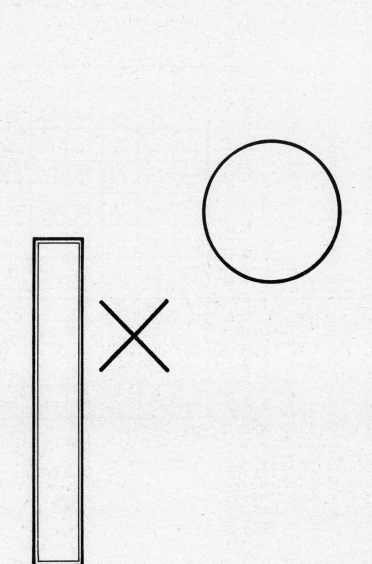

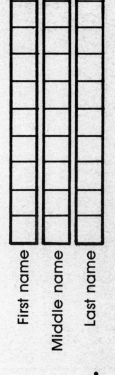

First name

Middle name

Last name

Last name first

RIDDLE PUZZLE

Name _____

Directions:

1. Count 5 rows down. Write the four-letter word starting in the 4th square.
2. Count 5 columns across. Reading down, write the word starting in the 5th square from the top.
3. Find the 10th column across. Write the word starting in the last 4 squares of this column.
4. Write the word made with every other letter in the second row down.
5. Count down to the 5th, 6th, and 7th rows. Write the word made from the 1st letter in each row.
6. Count across to the 9th column. Write the five-letter word that begins with the 1st letter in this column.

Do you know the answer to the riddle? If not, follow these directions.

1. Write the 1st letter in the 2nd row from the bottom.
2. Write the seven-letter word that is in the 4th row down, beginning in the 3rd square.
3. Find the 7th column across. Write the word that begins with the 5th letter in this column.

T	H	I	N	T	S	Q	U	F	E	L
W	O	H	O	E	H	E	T	L	M	S
O	P	E	N	R	G	B	D	I	X	E
Z	E	G	A	R	B	A	G	E	T	R
A	C	O	W	H	A	T	E	S	O	I
N	E	B	S	A	R	R	T	U	V	P
D	L	E	K	S	O	U	P	M	F	E
E	T	R	I	P	L	C	L	A	O	K
A	S	Q	W	A	L	K	O	R	U	N
L	A	W	G	M	A	N	T	K	R	O

Write the words you find here: _____

_____

For fun:

There are at least 21 words hidden in the rows and 21 words hidden in the columns, besides the words you just wrote. Can you find them?

"Following Directions," page 2; Solution, page 191.

MAP FILL-IN

Name _____

1. Read all the directions below before starting to fill in the map.
2. Use color and symbols to show:
   a river running from north to south
   two roads crossing the river
   two bridges for the roads
   a large swamp area between the two roads, east of the river
   an airport in the southeast
   a town on the western bank of the river, south of the southernmost road
   a church northwest of the northernmost road
   a mountain range west of the river
   a school west of the town
   two streams running from the mountain range into the river
3. Complete the legend to show what the colors and symbols on your map stand for.

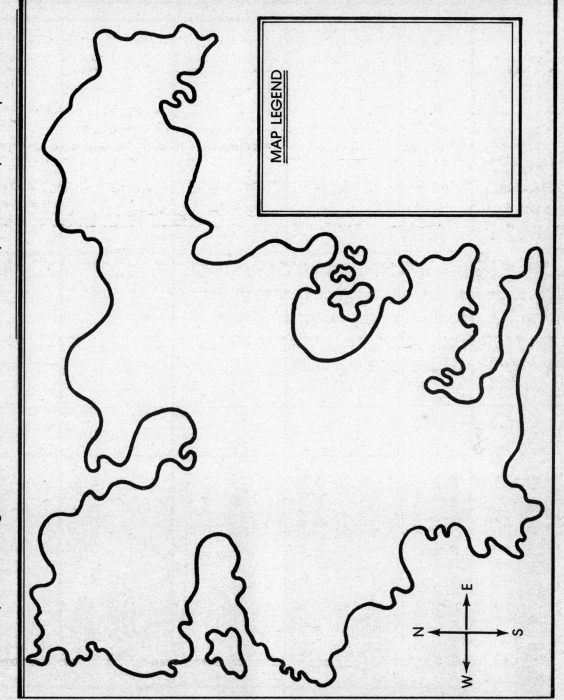

MAP LEGEND

"Following Directions," page 2; Solution, page 192.

Name _____

FOLLOWING DIRECTIONS BY MYSELF

Choose a book or other resource that gives directions for completing these tasks	List the source of the directions you followed	Date completed	Verbs used in the directions
Do a science experiment.			
Cook something from a recipe.			
Do an arts and crafts project.			
Go someplace using someone else's directions.			
Demonstrate a first-aid procedure.			
Fill out a form.			

"Following Directions," page 6; Solution, page 192.

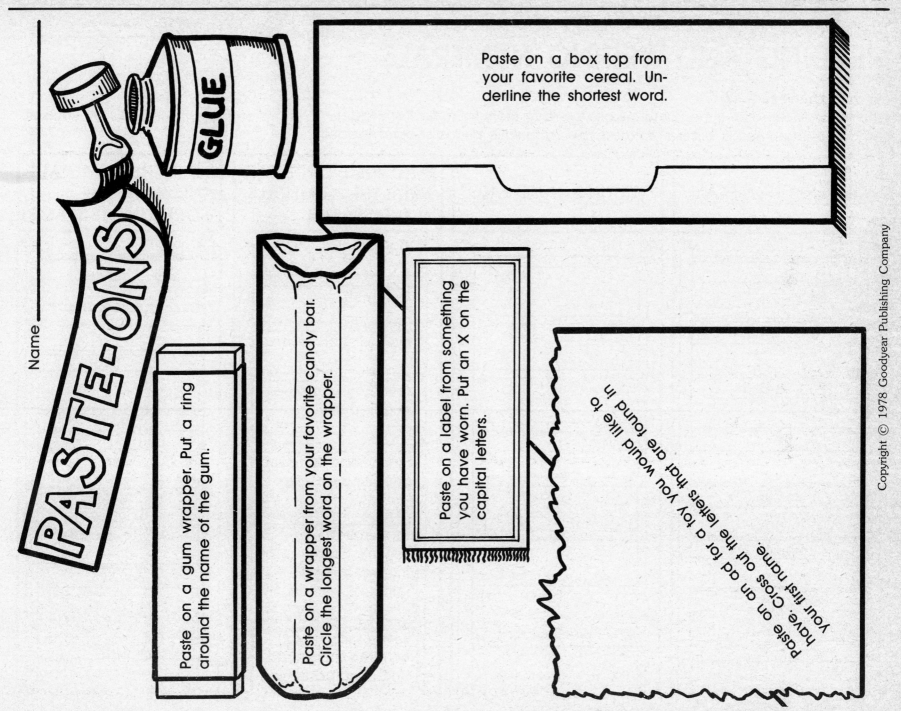

Name

GLUE

PASTE-ONS

Paste on a box top from your favorite cereal. Underline the shortest word.

Paste on a gum wrapper. Put a ring around the name of the gum.

Paste on a wrapper from your favorite candy bar. Circle the longest word on the wrapper.

Paste on a label from something you have worn. Put an X on the capital letters.

Paste on an ad for a toy you would like to have. Cross out the letters that are found in your first name.

"Following Directions," page 6.

READING AND WRITING NUMERALS

Name _____

To do with the teacher:
The teacher will check the numerals as you read them from the first ladder.
A new set of numerals will be dictated for you to write on the second ladder.

To do by yourself:
Complete these tasks by yourself.

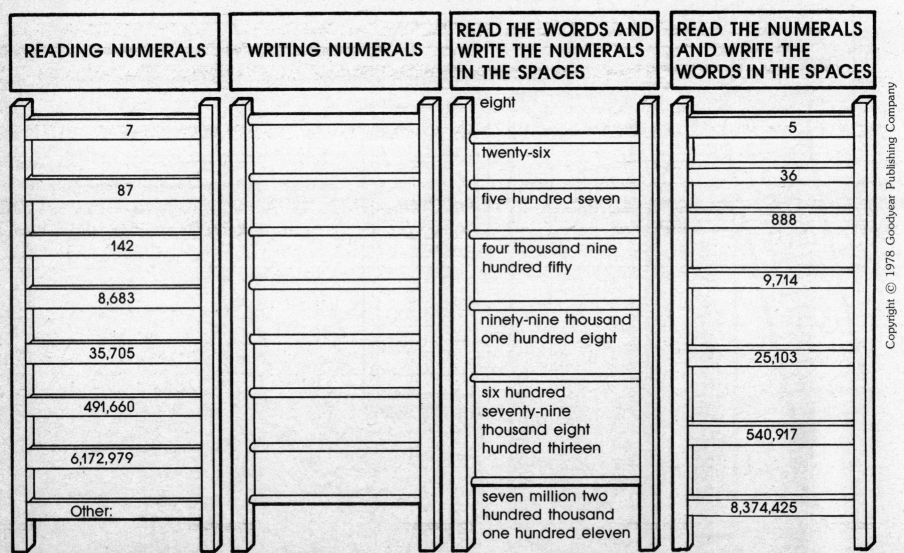

READING NUMERALS	WRITING NUMERALS	READ THE WORDS AND WRITE THE NUMERALS IN THE SPACES	READ THE NUMERALS AND WRITE THE WORDS IN THE SPACES
7		eight	5
87		twenty-six	36
142		five hundred seven	888
8,683		four thousand nine hundred fifty	9,714
35,705		ninety-nine thousand one hundred eight	
491,660		six hundred seventy-nine thousand eight hundred thirteen	25,103
6,172,979			540,917
Other:		seven million two hundred thousand one hundred eleven	8,374,425

"Reading and Writing Numerals," page 7; Solution, page 192.

SIZABLE SUMS

Name _____

Write the sums in number words

Show your work here in numerals

1. ten thousand four hundred
   plus
   eighty-five
   equals _____

2. six hundred fifty-seven
   plus
   one hundred thirty-two
   equals _____

3. nine hundred twenty-three million two
   hundred seventy-one thousand sixty-six
   plus
   ten million five thousand eight hundred ten
   equals _____

4. four hundred billion twelve million
   three thousand six hundred thirty-two
   plus
   one billion ten million one thousand two hundred two
   equals _____

5. nine hundred forty billion thirty-six million
   seven hundred twenty-five thousand four
   plus
   one million two hundred three
   thousand nine hundred thirteen
   equals _____

"Reading and Writing Numerals," page 9; Solution, page 192.

Name _____

NUMBER POEM

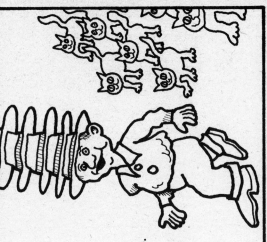

I once met a man on his way to St. Ives,
He had two thousand four hundred ninety-two wives.

One thousand two cats,
Six hundred three hats,
And two hundred thirty-six one-eyed bats.

He carried a pail of two thousand ten frogs,
And was chased by one hundred twenty-three dogs.
His seventeen sons wore eighty-five shirts,
And his daughter wore five hundred forty-eight skirts.

They all did arrive
In the town of St. Ives,
And forever after lived wonderful lives.

Write the numerals to tell how many of the things below are in the poem:

_____ wives   _____ hats   _____ frogs

_____ cats   _____ bats   _____ dogs

_____ sons   _____ shirts   _____ skirts

_____ daughters

List and find the total number of:

PEOPLE   ANIMALS   CLOTHES

"Reading and Writing Numerals," page 9; Solution, page 193.

14	7	21	6	9	13	52	3	25	37	38	11

Name _____

FOLDING FAN FORTUNES

Make a number fortune fan.

1. Write a fortune for each numeral on the fan. In the fortune, rewrite the numeral as a number word.
2. Fold the fan on the dotted lines.
3. Have a friend pick a number and tell your friend's fortune.

"Reading and Writing Numerals," page 9; Solution, page 193.

BASIC NUMBER FACTS

Use the code to record students' readiness, practice, and mastery of basic facts related to the various math processes.

CODE	
⊠ (diagonal)	indicates readiness
⊠ (X)	indicates student is studying or practicing; enter date when mastery is achieved

STUDENTS' NAMES	SKILLS											
	+			**−**			**×**			**÷**		
	BASIC FACTS (through 18)	SOLVING WORD PROBLEMS	APPLYING FACTS TO NEW SITUATIONS	BASIC FACTS (through 18)	SOLVING WORD PROBLEMS	APPLYING FACTS TO NEW SITUATIONS	BASIC FACTS (through 10's)	SOLVING WORD PROBLEMS	APPLYING FACTS TO NEW SITUATIONS	BASIC FACTS (dividends to 100)	SOLVING WORD PROBLEMS	APPLYING FACTS TO NEW SITUATIONS

"Basic Math Facts," page 13.

Name _____

JEOPARDY

To use as a worksheet for one person:

For each topic, write a related word problem and number equation in the boxes. The answers will be the numbers in the boxes.

To use as a game: (4 players)

1. Three of the players are contestants and the fourth is the moderator.
2. Each contestant selects a topic and writes word problems and equations for each numeral in his or her column. When a contestant completes a column, the moderator verifies the problems.
3. Contestants who correctly use all the numerals in their columns win.

FOOD	animals	CARS
6	4	2
8	9	10
10	14	16
81	24	36

"Basic Math Facts," page 14; Solution, page 193.

THE PYRAMID GAME

Name _____

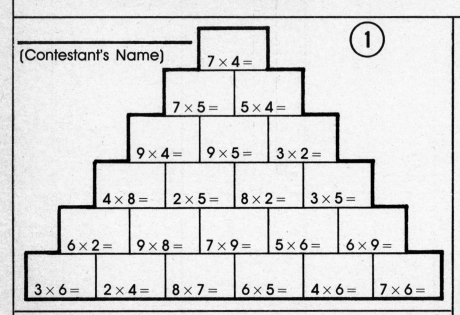

(1)

(Contestant's Name) _____

$7 \times 4 =$

$7 \times 5 =$ $5 \times 4 =$

$9 \times 4 =$ $9 \times 5 =$ $3 \times 2 =$

$4 \times 8 =$ $2 \times 5 =$ $8 \times 2 =$ $3 \times 5 =$

$6 \times 2 =$ $9 \times 8 =$ $7 \times 9 =$ $5 \times 6 =$ $6 \times 9 =$

$3 \times 6 =$ $2 \times 4 =$ $8 \times 7 =$ $6 \times 5 =$ $4 \times 6 =$ $7 \times 6 =$

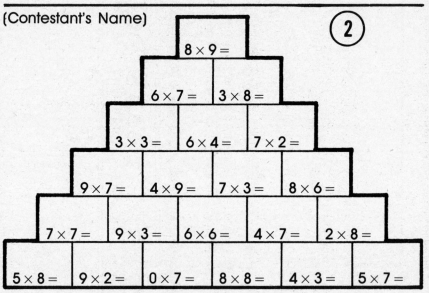

(2)

(Contestant's Name) _____

$8 \times 9 =$

$6 \times 7 =$ $3 \times 8 =$

$3 \times 3 =$ $6 \times 4 =$ $7 \times 2 =$

$9 \times 7 =$ $4 \times 9 =$ $7 \times 3 =$ $8 \times 6 =$

$7 \times 7 =$ $9 \times 3 =$ $6 \times 6 =$ $4 \times 7 =$ $2 \times 8 =$

$5 \times 8 =$ $9 \times 2 =$ $0 \times 7 =$ $8 \times 8 =$ $4 \times 3 =$ $5 \times 7 =$

To use as a worksheet for one person:
Fill in each pyramid with the correct products.

To use as a game: (3 players)
1. Get a stack of flashcards and a timer.
2. Write each player's name in one of the pyramid squares.
3. Choose a contestant, a tester, and a recorder.
4. Set the timer for two, three, or four minutes.
5. The tester shows flashcards to the contestant. For every correct answer the contestant gives, the recorder marks an X in a box of the contestant's pyramid. (Disregard the facts written on the worksheet.)
6. At the end of the time limit the next player becomes the contestant, and so on.
7. When all three players have had their turn as contestant, the one who has the most boxes in the pyramid filled in is the winner.

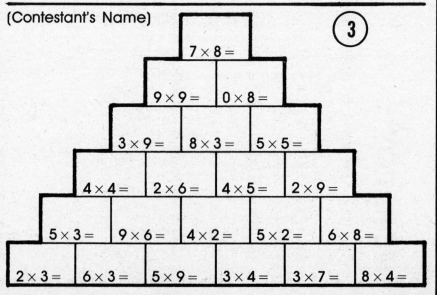

(3)

(Contestant's Name) _____

$7 \times 8 =$

$9 \times 9 =$ $0 \times 8 =$

$3 \times 9 =$ $8 \times 3 =$ $5 \times 5 =$

$4 \times 4 =$ $2 \times 6 =$ $4 \times 5 =$ $2 \times 9 =$

$5 \times 3 =$ $9 \times 6 =$ $4 \times 2 =$ $5 \times 2 =$ $6 \times 8 =$

$2 \times 3 =$ $6 \times 3 =$ $5 \times 9 =$ $3 \times 4 =$ $3 \times 7 =$ $8 \times 4 =$

"Basic Math Facts," page 15; Solution, page 193.

Name _____

IT'S THE REAL THING

1. Get a real six-pack container, muffin tin, pair of gloves, and egg carton.
2. Write math signs (+, −, ×, ÷) on the drawings below to show the kinds of basic facts you will make.
3. Group real objects (buttons, beans, bottle tops) in the containers to show all the ways you can make that number.
4. Write equations for each number name you discover on the lines beside the drawings.

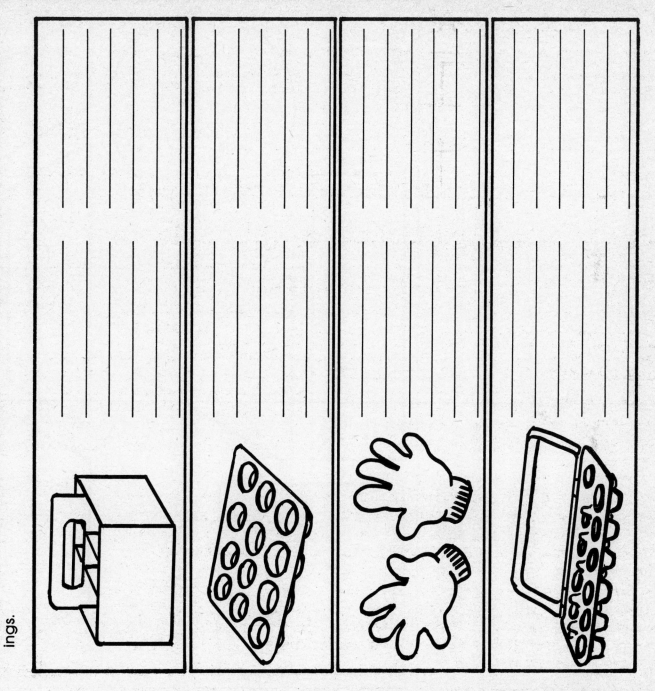

"Basic Math Facts," page 18; Solution, page 194.

Name

SHAPES

To the teacher:
Star one or more activities for children to do.

Do the activities that your teacher has starred for you.
Write your answers inside the shapes.
Label each shape.
Measure the area of each shape.
Mark all oblique angles with green, all obtuse angles with red,
all right angles with yellow.

"Geometry," page 19; Solution, page 194.

Name

COLOR THE SHAPES

See how many of these shapes you can find: triangle, square, rectangle, trapezoid, pentagon, parallelogram, hexagon, octagon. It's possible to find at least one of each. Color each type of shape with a different color.

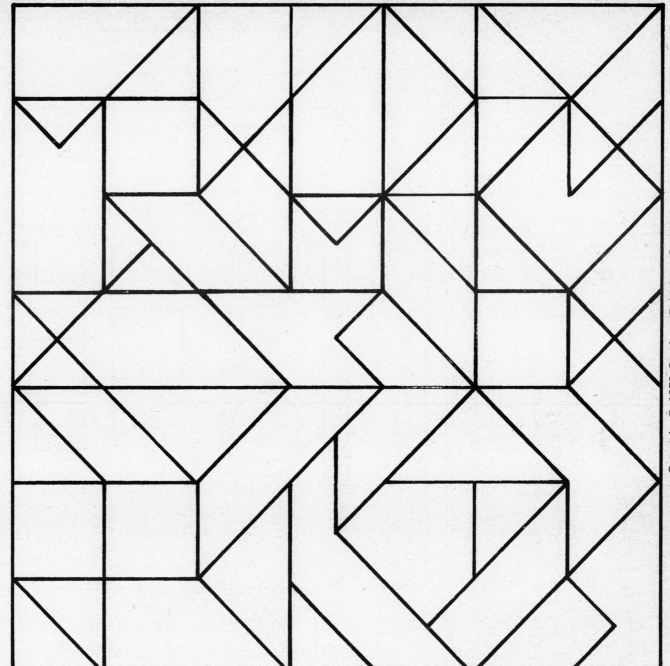

"Geometry," page 21; Solution, page 194.

SHAPE FACE

Do one of these activities:
List the kind and number of shapes.
Find the area of each quadrilateral.
Find the area of each enclosed shape.

Option:
Find a picture of a human or animal face.
Redraw the face using geometric shapes for the facial features.

Name

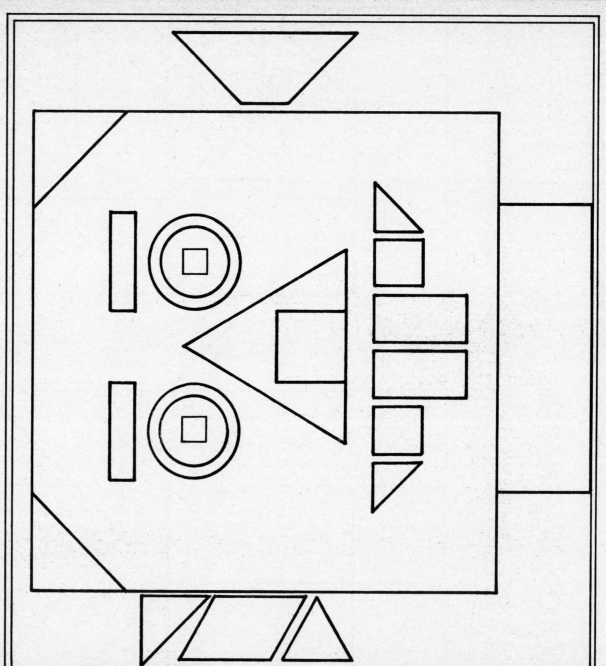

"Geometry," page 24; Solution, page 194.

WORD FAMILIES/RHYMING WORDS

1. Present words from the various word families for children to read.

2. Dictate words from the various word families for children to spell.

STUDENTS' NAMES	1. CAN READ																	2. CAN SPELL																
	at	it	an	ight	ate	ought	able	ack	ong	eet	ake	ouse	ook	ain	ee	ore		at	it	an	ight	ate	ought	able	ack	ong	eet	ake	ouse	ook	ain	ee	ore

"Word Families/Rhyming Words," page 25.

THE ITY CITY

Name _____

Write words on the things in the city.

"Word Families/Rhyming Words," page 27; Solution, page 195.

BLANKETY-BLANK-BLANK

Name _____

Complete each poem shown below.
1. Use the WORD LIST boxes to make lists of rhyming words for your poem.
2. Words on the same kind of lines must rhyme.
3. Words on each line must fit the clue written under the line.

POEM #1: NONSENSE

This poem doesn't need to make a lot of sense.

_____ _____
any word   any word

_____
any word

How can you _____ ?
          a verb

Change the vowel(s)

to make it _____
          any word

_____ _____
any word   any word

WORD LISTS
for Poem #1

POEM #2: PEOPLE POEM

_____ _____
person's name person's name

and _____
    person's name

went to the _____
            a place

_____ _____
person's name person's name

and _____
    person's name

saw the _____
        a thing

WORD LISTS
For Poem #2

POEM #3: A LOONY LIMERICK

This poem follows all of the rules, except that the words you write in the boxes do not need to rhyme with each other or with any other word in the poem.

The ~~~~

The ~~~~

WORD LISTS
for Poem #3

"Word Families/Rhyming Words," page 27; Solution, page 195.

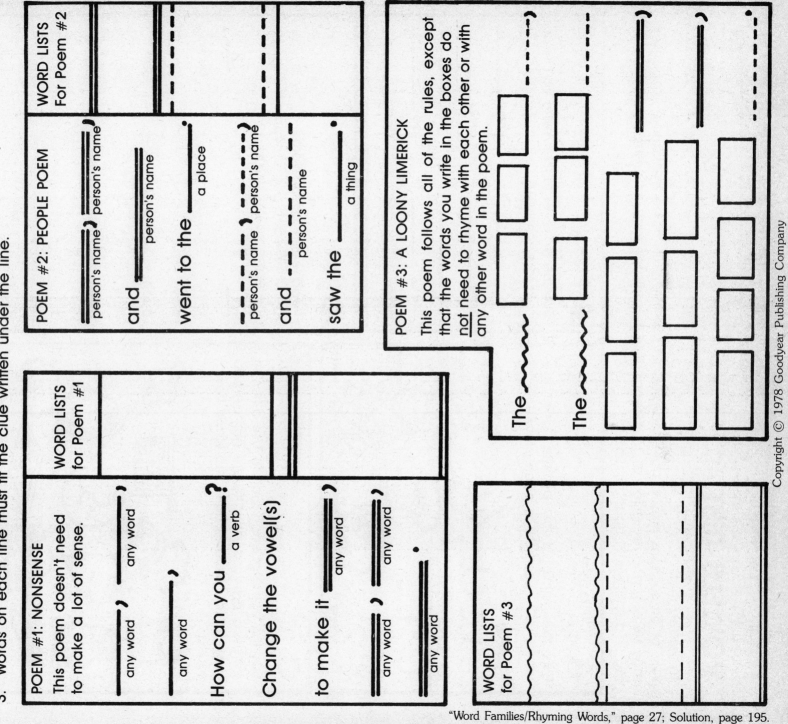

Name _____

VOWELS TEST

To the teacher:

Any or all sections may be used, depending on the skills to be evaluated. Responses may be oral and recorded by teacher or aide, or children may write responses according to directions in each section.

A

Say the name of the picture. Write the vowel you hear next to each picture.

B

Say the word. Write the vowel you hear next to each word.

hit _____   knee _____

hate _____   mop _____

foe _____   gum _____

use _____   ice _____

clap _____   bed _____

C

Say the name of each picture. Use different colored crayons or different numbers to show which pictures have the same vowel sound.

D

Read each list of words. Draw a line between each pair of words that have the same vowel sound.

1	2
shirt	plow
day	bought
ouch	Bert
flaw	soil
look	could
toy	cute
few	steer
toad	soul
thread	said
ear	weigh

"Vowels," page 31; Solution, page 195.

ANATOMY OF A VOWEL

Name _____

Directions:
1. Use this worksheet with your reading book or some other written material.
2. Write in words from your reading that have the same sound and spelling pattern as the words that label each body part.
3. Read the words you listed to a friend.

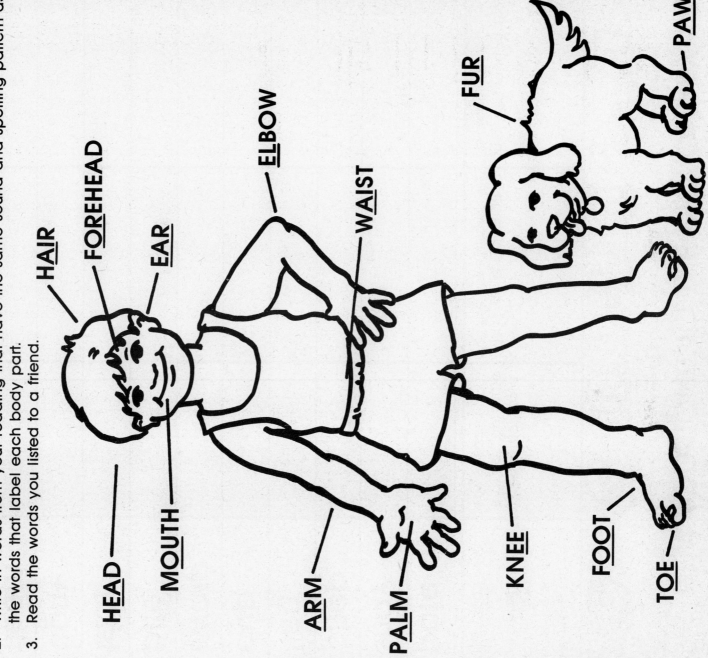

HAIR

FOREHEAD

EAR

HEAD

MOUTH

ELBOW

WAIST

ARM

PALM

KNEE

FOOT

TOE

FUR

PAW

"Vowels," page 32; Solution, page 195.

NEW ADDITIONS TO THE DICTIONARY

Follow the directions at the top of each column to complete the worksheet.

Name _____

Use these marks to show the sounds of the vowels in the words below: ⎯ long ˘ short ✗ silent	Write a real word that has the same vowel sound	Make up a definition for the "new" word	Use the "new" word in a sentence to show its meaning							
pote										
shay										
chep										
lieg										
dup										
swaip										
bife										
teap										
com										
fleem										
loak										
dind										

"Vowels," page 32; Solution, page 196.

WRITING SENTENCES

Have each student write sentences in WRITING SAMPLE/PRE-TEST, or attach sample sentences from his or her work. Enter comments below. After instruction and practice, repeat for the WRITING SAMPLE/POST-TEST.

Student's Name _____

WRITING SAMPLE/PRE-TEST

Date _____

WRITING SAMPLE/POST-TEST

Date _____

CHECKLIST

Items	Comments/Pre-Test	Comments/Post-Test
Fragments		
Run-ons		
Vocabulary Interesting adjectives, adverbs		
Interesting verbs (uses synonyms for such words as "said," "ran," etc.)		
Other		

"Writing Sentences," page 37.

SENTENCE FRAGMENTS/PICTURE FRAGMENTS

Name _____

The following sentences and pictures are incomplete. Beginnings, middles, or ends are missing. Fill in the missing parts of the sentences (with words) and pictures (with drawings).

by the sea.

We played and

Soda pop fizzled

The beautiful green snake

red ribbon on the package.

down the street.

through the clouds.

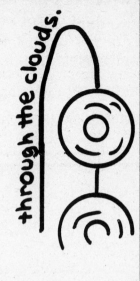

The pilot

Name _____

REARRANGING SENTENCES

The order of the words in our sentences is very important to what we want to say and how we want it to sound.

Play around with the order of each set of words to develop as many sentences that "make sense" as you can.

You can cut out and move words around, if you wish.

You must add punctuation to your finished sentences.

You may form questions.

Use all words in each set in each sentence you make up.

SET 1: Sam a runner is fast

_____

_____

SET 2: a dog brown saw a little the cat ball with

_____

_____

SET 3: silly over boy jumped elephant fat the the

_____

_____

SET 4: spaceship meteor the flash with in a a silver collided glowing

_____

_____

Can you fill the back of this page with at least four more sentences for each set?

| Sam | a | runner | is | fast |

a	dog	brown	saw	a
little	the	cat
ball	with

| silly | over | boy | jumped |
| elephant | fat | the | the |

spaceship	meteor	the
flash	with	in	a	a
silver	collided	glowing

"Writing Sentences," page 38; Solution, page 196.

SENTENCE EXPANDER

Name_____

Directions:
Read sentence 1 in part A. In the empty boxes write two words to tell what kind of monster.
In sentence 2, the new words you add will tell what kind of boy.
In sentence 3, your new words will tell where the monster was or what the monster was doing.
Expand the sentences in parts B and C, just like you did in part A.

Example:

Expand sentences.
You can expand sentences.
You can expand sentences to make them more interesting.

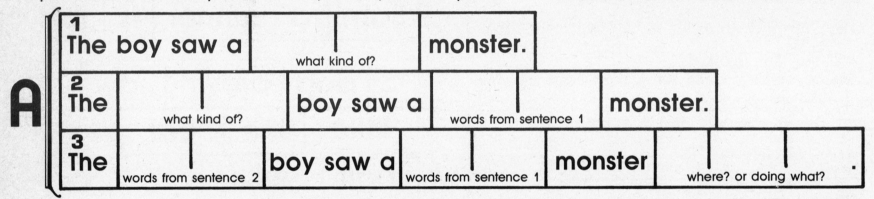

A

1 The boy saw a | what kind of? | monster.

2 The | what kind of? | boy saw a | words from sentence 1 | monster.

3 The | words from sentence 2 | boy saw a | words from sentence 1 | monster | where? or doing what? | .

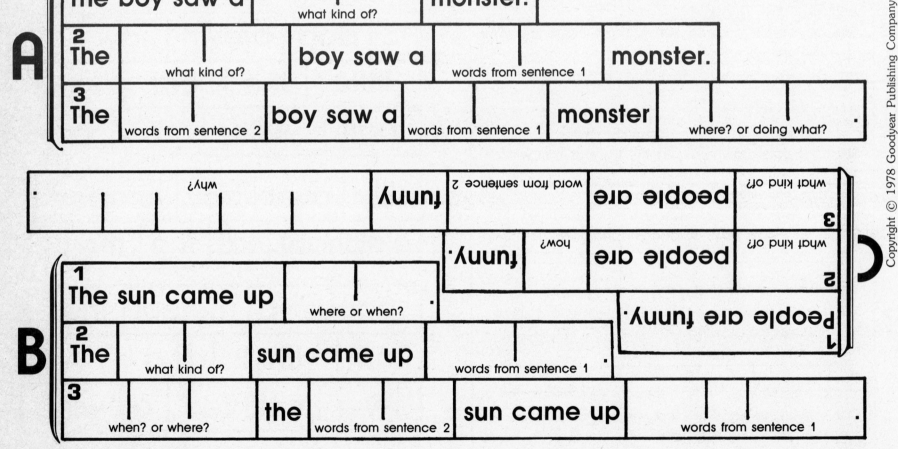

C

3 | what kind of? | people are | word from sentence 2 | funny | why? | .

2 | what kind of? | people are | how? | funny.

1 People are funny.

B

1 The sun came up | where or when? | .

2 The | what kind of? | sun came up | words from sentence 1 | .

3 | when? or where? | the | words from sentence 2 | sun came up | words from sentence 1 | .

Copyright © 1978 Goodyear Publishing Company

"Writing Sentences," page 39; Solution, page 196.

PUNCTUATION POWER

7. Pardon me Peter Piper said I need to put my peppers here

6. Peter Pipers pockets were full of picked pickled peppers

5. Help me pick peppers said Peter Piper

4. Peter also picked potatoes peas petunias parsley and pears

3. Fantastic Forty-two pecks of peppers

2. How many pecks did Peter Piper pick

1. Peter Piper picked a peck of pickled peppers

Directions:
Punctuate each sentence, from easy to difficult. Color in the scale to show your punctuation power.

Name _____

DIFFICULT

EASY

"Punctuation," page 43; Solution, page 197.

Name _____

PUNCTUATION PATTERNS

Fill in the blanks with words to make sentences that use the punctuation marks correctly.

1. _____ . _____ . _____ . _____ .

2. _____ ? _____ , _____ " _____

3. _____ " , _____ . _____ . _____ .

4. _____ . _____ . _____ . _____ .

5. _____ . _____ ! _____

6. _____ " _____ , _____ . _____

7. _____ " _____ ? " _____ ? " _____

8. _____ . _____ . _____ . _____

9. _____ " . _____ . _____ .

10. _____ ! _____ ! _____ !

"Punctuation," page 45; Solution, page 197.

Name _____

BOTHERSOME BUGS

DIRECTIONS

Cut out the bug body parts.
Match the bug body parts to form complete sentences.
Glue completed bugs on a piece of paper.
Make up some of your own bothersome bugs,
using the same punctuation marks.

France, Germany, and Greece.

I don't know

however, hostile natives
forced it
back to port.

The ocean liner
set sail for France

I won't say.

We visited the following countries

and can
travel a
long way
without water.

see the
enclosed photo

The camels in Egypt
have two humps

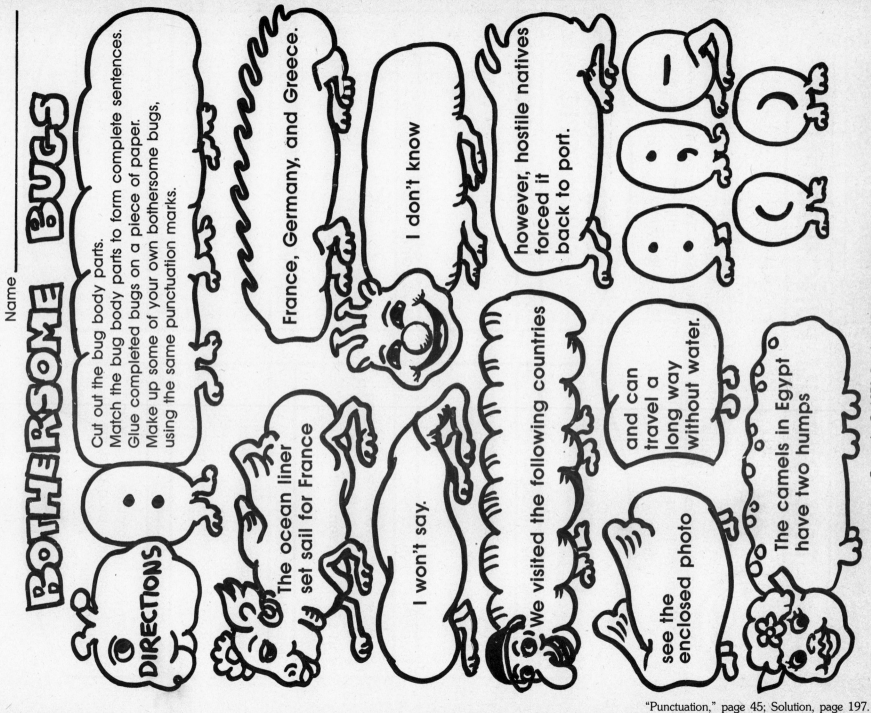

"Punctuation," page 45; Solution, page 197.

TIME CAPSULE PUNCTUATION

Correct the sentences in the Time Capsule by adding punctuation marks and capital letters where they are needed.

Choose a topic to research. Fill in each Time Zone with facts about your topic. Leave out the punctuation marks and capitals. Give it to a friend to correct.

INDEPENDENT STUDY TOPIC

TIME ZONE:

TIME ZONE:

TIME ZONE:

TIME ZONE:

PRESIDENTS

TIME ZONE: 1932

which president said a chicken in every pot

TIME ZONE: 1795–1799

at mt vernon george washington bred horses and cattle raised fruit and practiced crop rotation

TIME ZONE: 1909–1913

president tafts bathtub made especially for him was large enough to hold three people

TIME ZONE: 1945–1953

truman was responsible for creating nato the marshall plan and the truman doctrine

"Punctuation," page 47; Solution, page 197.

Name _____

PUNCTUATION P's AND Q's

Use the punctuation marks and words to make sentences. Add any other words or punctuation marks you need.

?	problem popular queer	.
!	quit phone poor	,
"	quiver quake prince	"
?	purple quart	,
!	quarantine queen parrot	.

Write your initials here: _____

Fill in each box with words that begin with your initials. Use the punctuation marks and words to make sentences. Add any other words or punctuation marks you need.

?	"	.
.	,	.
.	,	.
?	i	i
"	,	"

"Punctuation," page 48; Solution, page 198.

PARTS OF SPEECH

To the teacher:
Write in an appropriate sentence.

DIAGNOSTIC SENTENCE: _____

_____

Have each student read the sentence. Then ask the child to point out a noun, tell what a noun does, and give several examples of other nouns. Check for understanding of other parts of speech in the same manner.

STUDENTS' NAMES	DATE	NOUN			ADJECTIVE			VERB			ADVERB			OTHER		
		Identifies in context	Defines purpose	Gives new examples	Identifies in context	Defines purpose	Gives new examples	Identifies in context	Defines purpose	Gives new examples	Identifies in context	Defines purpose	Gives new examples	Identifies in context	Defines purpose	Gives new examples

"Parts of Speech," page 49.

USE YOUR NAME

Name _____

Directions:
1. Spell out your name in the boxes across the top.
2. Under each letter, write parts of speech that begin with that letter. Use adjectives that modify the nouns and adverbs that modify the verbs you've written for each letter.
3. Write a sentence for each group of words in a column. You will need to add other words and punctuation.

NOUN								
ADJECTIVE								
VERB								
ADVERB								

"Parts of Speech," page 50; Solution, page 198.

Name _____

PARTS-OF-SPEECH DOMINOES

Directions:

1. Cut out the word dominoes.
2. Paste them in the space below in a domino pattern. The sides of the dominoes that touch must be the same part of speech—noun, verb, adjective, or adverb.
3. On the blank half of any domino write in a word to make the parts of speech match.

START HERE:

big	sing

swim		blue		very	

tree		sun		man	

gaily		down		that	

"Parts of Speech," page 50; Solution, page 198.

USING
THE DICTIONARY

Name _____

Beginning Time _____

Ending Time _____

TEACHER'S COMMENTS

MY WORK

1. Circle the pair of guide words that would be listed on the page where these words are found.

   raccoon – rabbit – razor

   race – reach

   spaghetti – shell – space

   smell – string

2. Look up these words. Write the definition for each.

   judge _____

   suddenly _____

   reimburse _____

3. Divide these words into syllables.

   habitat _____

   peppermint _____

   society _____

4. Rewrite each list in alphabetical order.

   fig _____   deer _____

   pear _____   dog _____

   berry _____   dime _____

   lemon _____   dozen _____

   orange _____   dial _____

5. Pronounce these words for the teacher.
   a. kee´-hohl   e. pou´-der
   b. fayz´   f. pĭk´-cher
   c. skĭp´-r   g. mär´-shen
   d. swahp´   h. ri-do͞os´

"Using the Dictionary," page 55; Solution, page 198.

Name _____

SENSIBLE SYNONYMS

Answer the questions using synonyms for the underlined words.

Example:
Would you <u>feign</u> sickness?
No, I would not pretend to be sick.

1. Would you <u>gawk</u> at an elephant in a tree?

2. Would eating a gallon of ice cream make you feel <u>ecstatic</u>?

3. How would you look if you were <u>morose</u>?

4. Are you in the mood for a <u>succulent</u> food?

5. What is the last thing you <u>imbibed</u> today?

6. Would a <u>humdrum</u> movie interest you?

7. Would you pull the hair of a <u>languid</u> bear?

8. Is a <u>potpourri</u> something to cook in?

9. Would you rather criticize an ostrich or <u>ostracize</u> a critic?

10. Why does the hound make that <u>guttural</u> sound?

"Using the Dictionary," page 56; Solution, page 199.

WORDS, WORDS, WORDS

Each time your shape appears you must fill it in with the information asked for. Some words you might like to use: novel, drone, produce, inducement.

TEAM MEMBERS: ○— □— △—

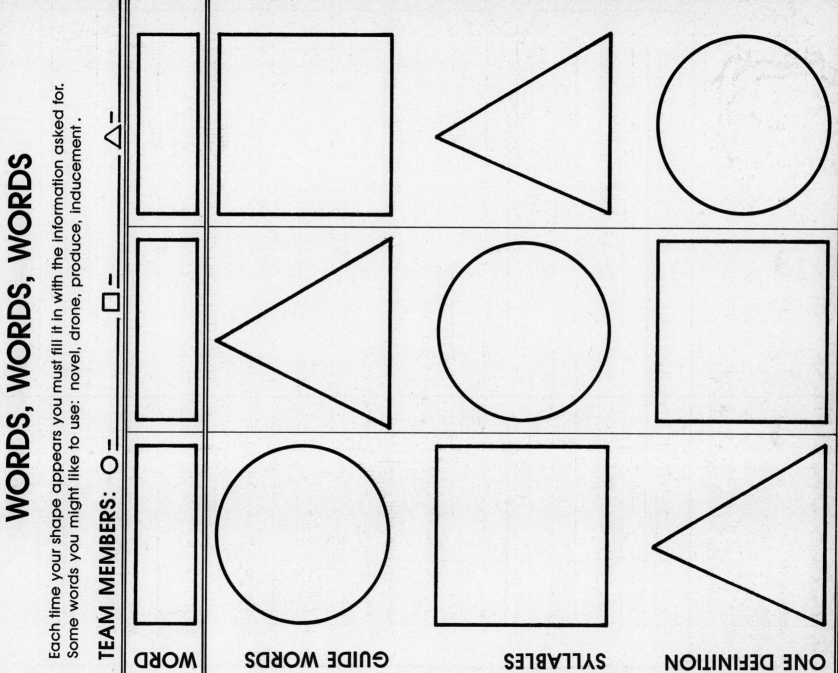

WORD

GUIDE WORDS

SYLLABLES

ONE DEFINITION

"Using the Dictionary," page 57; Solution, page 199.

DESIGN A DICTIONARY PAGE

Name _____

Directions:
1. Select nine words for your dictionary page.
2. Complete the worksheet by including all the parts used in a dictionary page, such as guide word, entry word, pronunciation, definition, illustration (for one of the words), and part of speech.

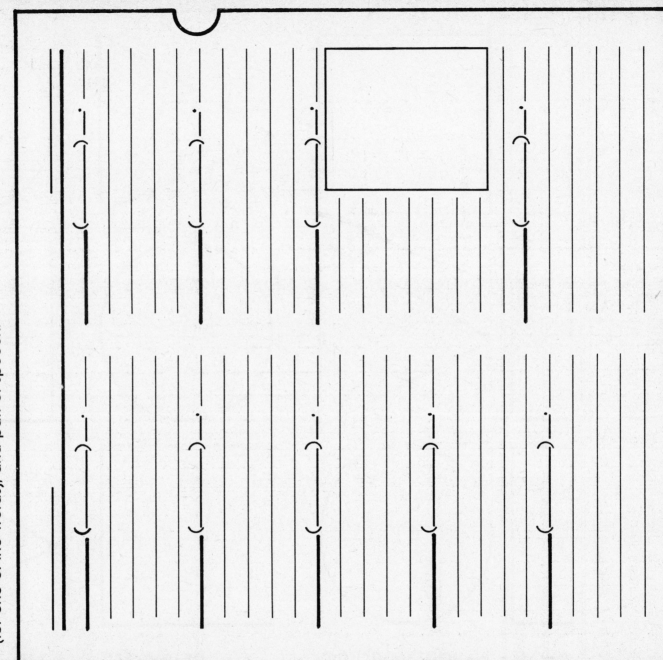

"Using the Dictionary," page 57; Solution, page 199.

PREFIXES AND SUFFIXES

Assess the children in a group activity, such as Pass the Hat (page 65), in the following way:

- ▨ not introduced to skill
- ◪ working on the skill
- ▰ mastery of the skill

STUDENTS' NAMES	Identifies prefixes in words	Defines prefixes	Gives words containing prefixes	Defines words containing prefixes	Uses words containing prefixes in a sentence	Knows these prefixes:	Identifies suffixes in words	Defines suffixes	Gives words containing suffixes	Defines words containing suffixes	Uses words containing suffixes in a sentence	Knows these suffixes:

"Prefixes and Suffixes," page 61.

PREFIX AND SUFFIX SERVICE, INC.

Directions:
Fill in the top of the worksheet. Use the information in the PART(S) and QUANTITY columns to make words. Write the words in the LABOR column. Note any spelling changes in the SERVICE column.

Name _____ Date _____

Address _____

City _____ State _____ Zip Code _____

Telephone _____

PART(S)	QUANTITY	LABOR	SERVICE
ANCE	2 words		
RE	3 words		
TION	6 words		
UN	4 words		
DIS, LY	5 words		
FUL	2 words		
SUB	3 words		
LESS	5 words		
ENT	2 words		

"Prefixes and Suffixes," page 62; solution, page 199.

Copyright © 1978 Goodyear Publishing Company

Name _____

AT YOUR SERVICE

Directions:

1. Write the name of a job or business you would like to have—for example, TV repairperson.

2. On the shapes below, write slogans or ads related to the job you chose, using as many words as you can that have prefixes and suffixes:

3. Underline or circle each prefix or suffix you use.

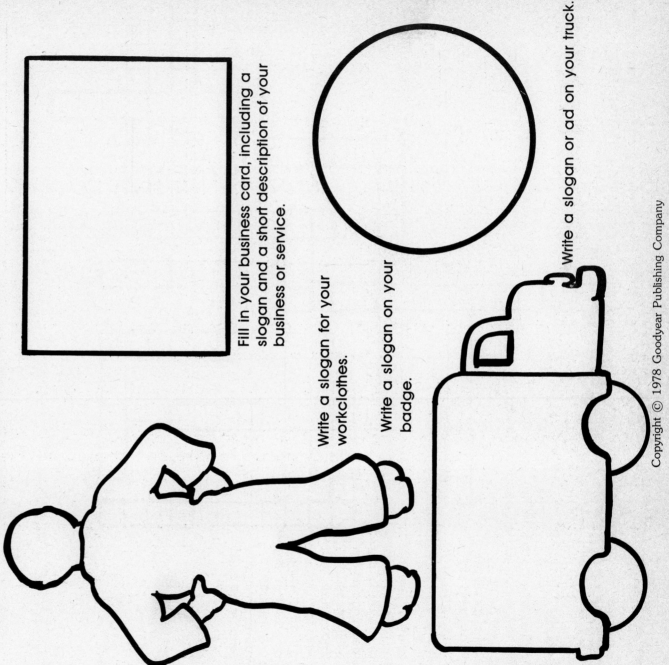

Fill in your business card, including a slogan and a short description of your business or service.

Write a slogan for your workclothes.

Write a slogan on your badge.

Write a slogan or ad on your truck.

"Prefixes and Suffixes," page 63; Solution, page 200.

Name _____

PREFIX/SUFFIX CROSSWORD

Directions:

Complete this puzzle in the usual way. Some new things you will need to know to complete it are:

1. Boxes for all pre-fixes and suf-fixes are out-lined in darker lines.

2. In the clues, the capital words tell you the meanings of the prefixes and suf-fixes that you will use.

3. All root words needed in the puzzle can be found in some form in the clue.

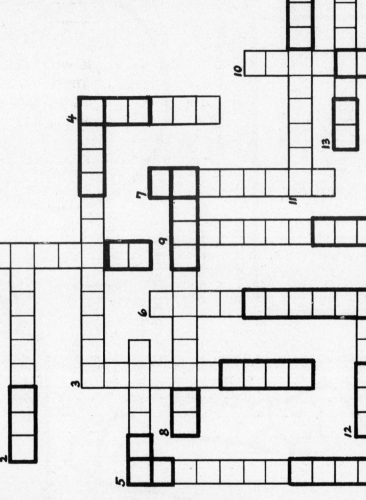

ACROSS

2. to TAKE AWAY or MOVE FROM the usual location
3. THE STATE OF being related
5. NOT at ease
8. NOT POSSIBLE to speak of
11. ACT OF being graduated
12. roadlike way that is UNDER ground
13. to catch IN a trap or snare

DOWN

1. TO MAKE more intense
3. ABLE to be resisted
4. to pay BEFORE
5. STATE OF BEING NOT happy
6. IN A MANNER INDICATING LACK OF fact
7. design AGAIN
9. FILLED WITH beauty
10. MANNER of being neat

"Prefixes and Suffixes," page 63; Solution, page 200.

GAME 1

sleepless understand uncover	helpful story unaware	outside rearrange partnership
displace exclamation butcher	rechargeable sidewalk unleash	forgetful discontent lumber
enjoyment repair parade	proclaim difference restaurant	snowman painless subhuman

PREFIX/SUFFIX TIC-TAC-TOE

Names _____ (player 1)

_____ (player 2)

Directions: (2 players)

In each game, decide who will be P and who will be S (flip a coin or draw). P marks prefixes; S marks suffixes. The youngest player begins the game.

1. Choose a square and find the word that contains your word part.
2. Read the word and spell the prefix or suffix.
3. If you are correct, the square is yours and you may mark it. If you are wrong, the square belongs to the other player.
4. Settle any disagreements with a dictionary.

Game 1 Winner _____

Game 2 Winner _____ Game 3 Winner_____

Copyright © 1978 Goodyear Publishing Company

GAME 2

coexist comfort disappearance	happiness rename purple	plastic decode fulfillment
cooperate painful product	distaste favorable recognize	reletter cupful relation
beside homeward direction	attempt homeless disbelief	return backward jingle

GAME 3

portion afterward preoccupy	restate fearless toothpaste	action inside retell
parlor kindness preview	bemoan armchair lamentable	playful liquid regain
playground undecidedly rejoin	promotion cowboy antifreeze	seasonal sportsmanship interact

"Prefixes and Suffixes," page 63. Solution, page 200.

MAIN IDEA

Name _____

I. Fill in the bubble that names the letter of the topic sentence.

A B C D E
○ ○ ○ ○ ○

A There are many different kinds and locations of homes. B Some homes are small. C Some homes are big. D Some homes are near the city. E Where do you live?

II. ✔ the number that matches the topic sentence.

___1 ___2 ___3 ___4

1 The rose is a flower that is often used for corsages. 2 The chrysanthemum is a flower that is eaten. 3 Some flowers are used to make teas. 4 Flowers are used for a variety of purposes.

III. Write the letter that names the topic sentence. _____

a Cinderella was crying. b Her stepsisters were angry. c Everyone in the house was upset. d The cat was running around. e The dog was barking.

IV. Write or tell your teacher the main idea of the picture in your own words.

_____
_____
_____
_____
_____

V. Write the main idea of the story in your own words.

_____
_____
_____
_____
_____

Mary had a dog as a pet. They played together. They watched TV together. They went everywhere together.

VI. List the key words of the paragraph below.

_____
_____
_____
_____

Names of fish often give clues to their many different shapes and colors. There are yellow-tail tunas and pink salmon. Can you guess the shapes of the pipefish and the hammerhead shark?

To the teacher:
Check the appropriate column to indicate the student's performance on these main-idea exercises.

ITEM	RESPONDED APPROPRIATELY	NEEDS PRACTICE
Locates topic sentence in context (I, II, III)		
States main idea from picture or paragraph (IV, V)		
Identifies key words (VI)		

"Main Idea/Summarizing," page 67; Solution, page 200.

Name _____

MAIN STREET

Directions:
For each Main Street, read a paragraph, chapter, or story. Write a key word from what you have read in each building. Use the key words to write a main-idea statement on Main Street.

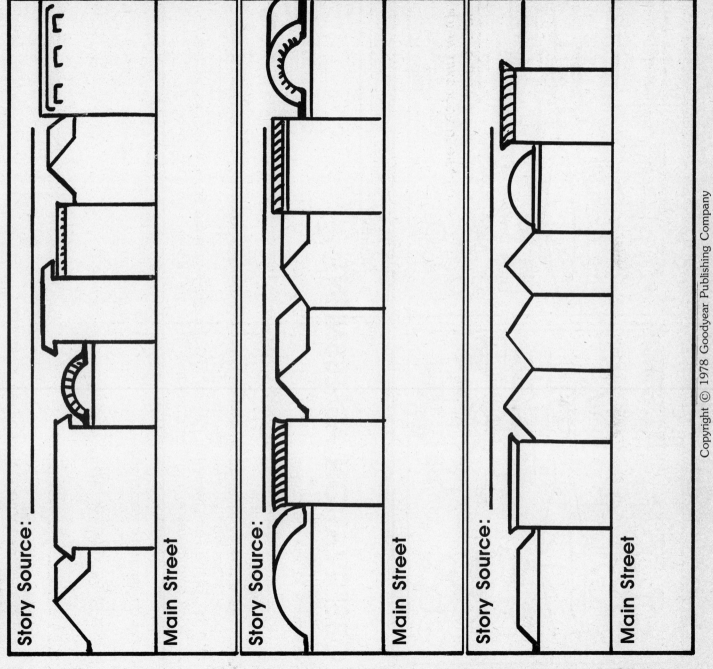

Story Source: _____

Main Street

Story Source: _____

Main Street

Story Source: _____

Main Street

"Main Idea/Summarizing," page 68; Solution, page 201.

OBSERVATION ASSESSMENT

Name _____

Questions to ask the student:

1. Look at picture A for one minute. Cover the picture and tell me everything you can remember about it.

2. Look at the Ferris wheel in picture A [or the merry-go-round or some other specific part]. What can you tell me about it?

3. Look at the Ferris wheel in picture B. Compare it with the Ferris wheel in picture A.

4. Look at pictures A and B and tell how they are different from each other.

Notes on student's responses:

1. Recalling visual details:

2. Observing details:

3, 4. Observing for likenesses and differences:

SCIENTIST'S LOG

Directions:
Choose something to observe. Fill in the log as you plan and make your observations. Some of the types of things you might observe are: a tree near the school; a cocoon; the sandbox area; a bulletin board; a flowering plant; the gutter in the street in front of the school; the lunch area.

OBSERVER'S NAME: _____

ITEM OR SITUATION UNDER OBSERVATION: _____

SITE OF OBSERVATION: _____

MATERIALS USED:
RULER _____ THERMOMETER _____ MICROSCOPE _____
MAGNIFYING GLASS _____ SCALE _____ CAMERA _____
BINOCULARS _____ OTHER _____

FIRST OBSERVATION (give a complete description of item or situation): _____

DATE: _____

LATER OBSERVATIONS (note changes observed):   DATES: _____

"Observation," page 74; Solution, page 201.

SENSES TAKING

Name _____

A trip to _____

In the first column, name the stops you make on your trip. In the other columns, describe what you see, hear, smell, taste, and feel at each stop.

STOPS YOU MAKE	👁	👂	👃	👄	✋

"Observation," page 78; Solution, page 201.

SEEING RELATIONSHIPS

Name _____

CATEGORIZING:
Put an X on the pictures that belong in the same group as a ball. These belong in the same group because _____

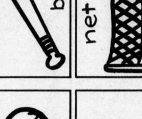 bat

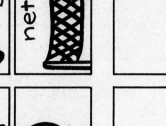 donut

 button

 net

 wheel

CATEGORIZING:
Add three more pictures that belong in the group. These belong in the group because _____

CAUSE AND EFFECT: Match each cause to its effect by drawing connecting lines.

CAUSES	EFFECTS
He put too much air in the ball.	The ball went into the stands.
The batter hit a home run.	He paid the man $50.00.
The golfer hit the ball into a window.	He had to buy a new ball.

SEQUENCE: Arrange the pictures in order by putting a number inside each picture.

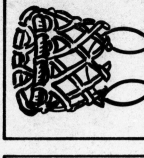

BRUINS **2** TROJANS **0**

OTHER RELATIONSHIPS: Teacher-designed activity to assess student's ability to understand other relationships such as time, place, and analogies.

"Seeing Relationships," page 79; Solution, page 201.

CLASSIFYING

Cut out the numbered squares. Lay out all the squares that go under column A and write the numbers under the column heading. Return these squares to the others. Now find all the squares for column B and write their numbers. Continue until you have completed all the columns.

ball 1.	2.	nail 3.	4.
5.	board 6.	7.	hockey puck 8.
9.	skis 10.	mitt 11.	cookie 12.
cow 13.	dime 14.	15.	16.
17.	knife 18.	19.	pie 20.
21.	22.	football 23.	24.

Name _____

A	B	C	D	E	F	G	H
round man-made things	sports things	wooden things	one-syllable words	rubber sports items	growing things	sharp metal things	things you wear on your hands

"Seeing Relationships," page 80; Solution, page 202.

Name _____

CAUSE-AND-EFFECT BINGO

To use as a worksheet for one person:
1. Find an effect to match each cause.
2. Indicate matching causes and effects with the same number. Use a new number for each pair you find.

	1	2	3	4	5
C		When the roller coaster sped down the steepest incline,	flood		earthquake
A			When he shook the pop bottle before opening it,	NO VACANCY	Because he found his lost dog,
U	FEB 5 JOHN'S BIRTHDAY	His fish was the largest caught for the day.	John carried the ball into the end zone.		FREE
S		FREE		springtime	OCT 31 HALLOWEEN
E	He didn't feed his goldfish		missed catching a fly ball		
E		smog	so they died.		everyone screamed.
F	The team scored six points.			a flat tire	the soda squirted out.
F		he was happy.	FREE		birds building nests, flowers blooming
E	The winner!		The boy was dressed as Dracula	1ST PRIZE	FREE
C		thunder		homeless people	error in baseball

"Seeing Relationships," page 81; Solution, page 202.

DRAWING CONCLUSIONS

Check the evidence that supports the conclusion.

CONCLUSION

The pet got out
of the cage.

EVIDENCE

___ the cage was empty.

___ The pet was hiding
under the newspaper
in the cage.

___ Nobody could find
the pet.

___ Everyone saw the
pet run away.

Write a conclusion for the evidence.

EVIDENCE

People were happy.

Cake was served.

Presents were opened.

Everyone sang.

CONCLUSION

_____

_____

_____

Match each conclusion with evidence.

CONCLUSION

Mickey Mouse
is Donald Duck's
friend.

Mickey Mouse
is famous.

Mickey Mouse
is a cartoon
character.

EVIDENCE

His picture is in
the Hall of Fame
and watches have his
picture on them.

He is drawn by
someone and
doesn't really talk.

He is shown holding
hands with him and
they play together.

Name _____

CHARACTER CONCLUSIONS

Directions:
1. Write the names of three characters from a story you've read.
2. Write in a feeling you think each character had at some time during the story.
3. List evidence from the story that seems to prove the character felt this way.

Story Title _____

Author _____

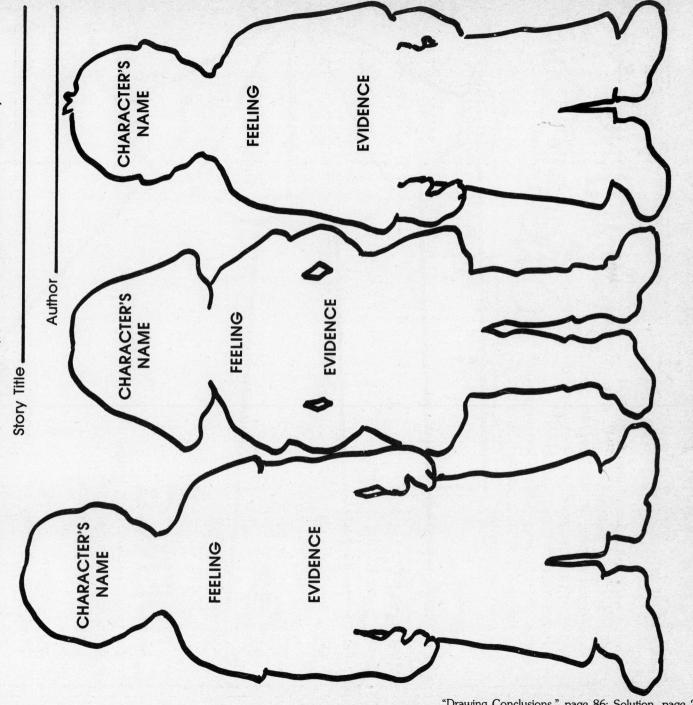

CHARACTER'S NAME

FEELING

EVIDENCE

CHARACTER'S NAME

FEELING

EVIDENCE

CHARACTER'S NAME

FEELING

EVIDENCE

"Drawing Conclusions," page 86; Solution, page 202.

HOPPING TO CONCLUSIONS

CONCLUSIONS

- she probably felt lonely
- it must have rained
- it was springtime
- it was a funny joke
- she had the measles

Directions:
1. Read a conclusion on the lily pad.
2. Read the list of evidence.
3. Mark the numbers on the jumping path that match the pieces of evidence needed to reach the conclusion.
4. Draw the jumping pattern the frog will use to get to the lily pad by connecting the numbers like this:

EVIDENCE

1. the lawn was wet and green
2. tears ran down her cheeks
3. air was fresh and clean
4. played by herself
5. wasn't allowed visitors
6. drops of water were on the flowers
7. couldn't wait to tell her brother
8. flowers blossomed
9. was visited by the doctor
10. no one was at her birthday party
11. dark clouds were in the sky
12. laughed and laughed
13. was covered with red spots
14. birds chirped in their nests
15. wished the other children would play with her

"Drawing Conclusions," page 86; Solution, page 203.

Name _____

DECISIONS, DECISIONS, DECISIONS

Directions:
1. Write in three of your family's decisions.
2. For each decision, tell how family members did — or did not — support the decision.

DECISION

Family Member	Supporting/Not Supporting the Decision

DECISION

Family Member	Supporting/Not Supporting the Decision

DECISION

Family Member	Supporting/Not Supporting the Decision

"Drawing Conclusions," page 90; Solution, page 203.

Name _____

BUSINESS CARD WORKSHEET

Check ✓ the activities you will do.

___ Design business cards for several of your own businesses (or pastimes).

___ Design cards for businesses or jobs you would like to have.

___ Design cards for friends and classmates describing talents and skills they have.

"Business Cards," page 97.

Name _____

GREETING CARD INVENTORY

Directions:
Take twenty to fifty greeting cards. Choose a category from the list below or make up your own. Sort the cards to fit the category and record the results on the graph.

CATEGORIES: Kinds of occasions (birthday, Halloween, Valentine's Day, Christmas, Hanukah, etc.); kinds of designs (flowers, abstract, cartoon, etc.); main colors used; sizes; prices; lettering style; names or types of people to receive the cards.

CATEGORY:						
1						
2						
3						
4						
5						
6						
7						
8						
9						
10						

"Greeting Cards," page 119.

FOLLOWING DIRECTIONS

1. Write your name in the upper right-hand corner. Circle the first and last letter. Write the date under your name.
2. Write your name on the line in the lower left-hand corner.
3. Write your first initial and your last name above the box in the upper left-hand corner.
4. Write your initials in the circle. Underline your last initial.
5. Write your name in capital letters in the boxes in the lower right-hand corner. Use one box for each letter. Color in any empty boxes.
6. Write your last name down the left-hand side and your first name down the right-hand side of the paper. Number each letter in your name.
7. Write your last name to the right of the X. Cross out every other letter.

Teacher option: Have student follow oral directions to
complete a task _____
go to a location _____

S. Smith

Sally Smith
Oct. 1

S 1
M 2
I 3
T 4
H 5

X Sally Smith

(S.K.S.)

6 S
7 A
8 L
9 L
10 Y

First name | S | A | L | L | Y
Middle name | K | A | Y
Last name | S | M | I | T | H

Smith, Sally
Last name first

"Following Directions," page 1.

RIDDLE PUZZLE

Name _____

Directions:
1. Count 5 rows down. Write the four-letter word starting in the 4th square.
2. Count 5 columns across. Reading down, write the word starting in the 5th square from the top.
3. Find the 10th column across. Write the word starting in the last 4 squares of this column.
4. Write the word made with every other letter in the second row down.
5. Count down to the 5th, 6th, and 7th rows. Write the word made from the 1st letter in each row.
6. Count across to the 9th column. Write the five-letter word that begins with the 1st letter in this column.

Do you know the answer to the riddle? If not, follow these directions.

1. Write the 1st letter in the 2nd row from the bottom.
2. Write the seven-letter word that is in the 4th row down, beginning in the 3rd square.
3. Find the 7th column across. Write the word that begins with the 5th letter in this column.

T H I N T S Q U F E L
W O O D O H O T O M S
O P E N R G B D I X E
Z E G A R B A G E T R
A C O W H A T E S O I
N E B S A R R T U V P
D L E K S O U P M F E
E T R I P L C L A O K
A S Q W A L K O R U N
L A W G M A N T K B O

Write the words you find here: what has four wheels, and
flies, a garbage truck

For fun:
There are at least 21 words hidden in the rows and 21 words hidden in the columns, besides the words you just wrote. Can you find them?

"Following Directions," page 2.

WORKSHEET SOLUTIONS

MAP FILL-IN

Name _____ JOHN

1. Read all the directions below before starting to fill in the map.
2. Use color and symbols to show:
   a river running from north to south
   two roads crossing the river
   two bridges for the roads
   a large swamp area between the two roads, east of the river
   an airport in the southeast
   a town on the western bank of the river, south of the southernmost road
   a church northwest of the northernmost road
   a mountain range west of the town
   a school west of the town
   two streams running from the mountain range into the river
3. Complete the legend to show what the colors and symbols on your map stand for.

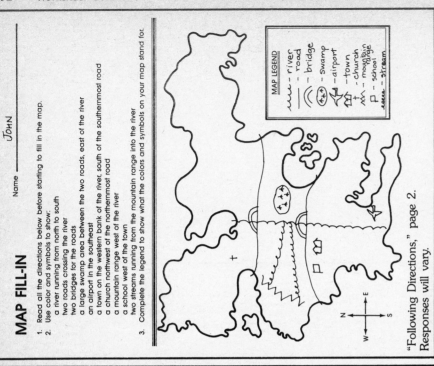

MAP LEGEND

~~~ – river
—– – road
)–(– bridge
)(·) – swamp
✈ – airport
◻ – town
† – church
⌃⌃⌃ – mountain
p – school
~~~ – stream

"Following Directions," page 2.
Responses will vary.

FOLLOWING DIRECTIONS BY MYSELF

Name _____ Sam Jones

Choose a book or other resource that gives directions for completing these tasks	List the source of the directions you followed	Date completed	Verbs used in the directions
Do a science experiment.	I did "Air Expansion" in Science for All, p. 37.	Mar. 12	heat blow up measure stretch
Cook something from a recipe.	I made brownies from Cooking for Kids, p. 121.	Mar. 18 Mrs. Jones	sift mix measure fold bake
Do an arts and crafts project.			
Go someplace using someone else's directions.	I followed my Dad's directions to the store.	Mar. 20 Mr. Jones	turn left go pass
Demonstrate a first-aid procedure.			
Fill out a form.			

"Following Directions," page 6.
Responses will vary.

READING AND WRITING NUMERALS

Name _____

To do with the teacher:
The teacher will check the numerals as you read them from the first ladder.
A new set of numerals will be dictated for you to write on the second ladder.

To do by yourself:
Complete these tasks by yourself.

READING NUMERALS	WRITING NUMERALS	READ THE WORDS AND WRITE THE NUMERALS IN THE SPACES	READ THE NUMERALS AND WRITE THE WORDS IN THE SPACES
7		eight 8	5 five
87		twenty-six 26	36 thirty-six
142		five hundred seven 507	888 eight hundred eighty-eight
8,683		four thousand nine hundred fifty 4,950	9,714 nine thousand seven hundred fourteen
35,705		ninety-nine thousand one hundred eight 99,108	25,103 twenty-five thousand one hundred three
491,660		six hundred seventy-nine thousand eight hundred thirteen 679,813	540,917 five hundred forty thousand nine hundred seventeen
6,172,979		seven million two hundred thousand one hundred eleven 7,200,111	8,374,425 eight million three hundred seventy-four thousand four hundred twenty-five
Other:			

"Reading and Writing Numerals," page 7.

SIZABLE SUMS

Name _____

Write the sums in number words. | Show your work here in numerals

1. ten thousand four hundred
   plus
   eighty-five
   equals
   ten thousand four hundred eighty-five

   ① 10,400
   + 85
   10,485

2. six hundred fifty-seven
   plus
   one hundred thirty-two
   equals
   seven hundred eighty-nine

   ② 657
   + 132
   789

3. nine hundred twenty-three million two
   hundred seventy-one thousand sixty-six
   plus
   ten million five thousand eight hundred ten
   equals
   nine hundred thirty-three million
   two hundred seventy-six thousand
   eight hundred seventy-six

   ③ 923,271,066
   + 10,005,810
   933,276,876

4. four hundred billion twelve million
   three thousand six hundred thirty-two
   plus
   one billion ten million one thousand two hundred two
   equals
   four hundred one billion twenty-two
   million four thousand eight
   hundred thirty-four

   ④ 400,012,003,632
   1,010,001,202
   401,022,004,834

5. nine hundred forty billion thirty-six million
   seven hundred twenty-five thousand four
   plus
   one million two hundred three thousand thirteen
   equals
   nine hundred forty billion thirty-
   seven million nine hundred twenty-
   eight thousand nine hundred seventeen

   ⑤ 940,036,725,004
   + 1,203,913
   940,037,928,917

"Reading and Writing Numerals," page 9.

NUMBER POEM

Name _____

I once met a man on his way to St. Ives,
He had two thousand four hundred ninety-two wives.

One thousand two cats,
Six hundred three hats,
And two hundred thirty-six one-eyed bats.

He carried a pail of two thousand ten frogs.
And was chased by one hundred twenty-three dogs.
His seventeen sons wore eighty-five shirts,
And his daughter wore five hundred forty-eight skirts.

They all did arrive
In the town of St. Ives,
And forever after lived wonderful lives.

Write the numerals to tell how many of the things below are in the poem:

2,492	wives	
1,002	cats	
603	hats	
236	bats	
2,010	frogs	
123	dogs	
85	shirts	
548	skirts	

List and find the total number of:

PEOPLE

1	man
2,492	wives
17	sons
1	daughter
2,511	people

ANIMALS

1,002	cats
236	bats
2,010	frogs
123	dogs
3,371	animals

CLOTHES

603	hats
85	shirts
548	skirts
1,236	pieces of clothing

"Reading and Writing Numerals," page 9.

FOLDING FAN FORTUNES

Name _____ Paul

Make a number fortune fan.

1. Write a fortune for each numeral on the fan. In the fortune, rewrite the numeral as a number word.
2. Fold the fan on the dotted lines.
3. Have a friend pick a number and tell your friend's fortune.

"Reading and Writing Numerals," page 9.
Responses will vary.

JEOPARDY

Name _____ Leslie

To use as a worksheet for one person:

For each topic, write a related word problem and number equation in the boxes. The answers will be the numbers in the boxes.

To use as a game: (4 players)

1. Three of the players are contestants and the fourth is the moderator.
2. Each contestant selects a topic and writes word problems and equations for each numeral in his or her column. When a contestant completes a column, the moderator verifies the problems.
3. Contestants who correctly use all the numerals in their columns win.

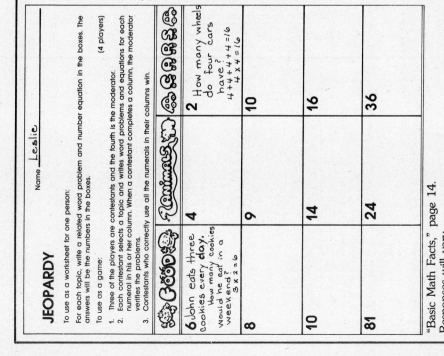

"Basic Math Facts," page 14.
Responses will vary.

THE PYRAMID GAME

Name _____

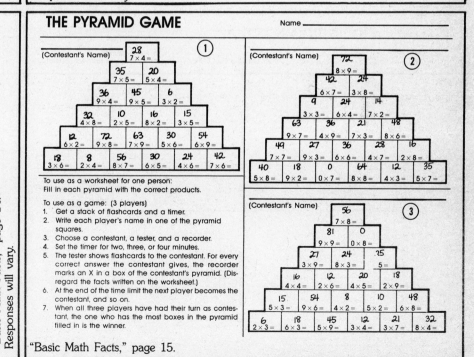

To use as a worksheet for one person:
Fill in each pyramid with the correct products.

To use as a game: (3 players)

1. Get a stack of flashcards and a timer.
2. Write each player's name in one of the pyramid squares.
3. Choose a contestant, a tester, and a recorder.
4. Set the timer for two, three, or four minutes.
5. The tester shows flashcards to the contestant. For every correct answer the contestant gives, the recorder marks an X in a box of the contestant's pyramid. (Disregard the facts written on the worksheet.)
6. At the end of the time limit the next player becomes the contestant, and so on.
7. When all three players have had their turn as contestant, the one who has the most boxes in the pyramid filled in is the winner.

"Basic Math Facts," page 15.

IT'S THE REAL THING

Name _____ Marcia

1. Get a real six-pack container, muffin tin, pair of gloves, and egg carton.
2. Write math signs (+, −, ×, ÷) on the drawings below to show the kinds of basic facts you will make.
3. Group real objects (buttons, beans, bottle tops) in the containers to show all the ways you can make that number.
4. Write equations for each number name you discover on the lines beside the drawings.

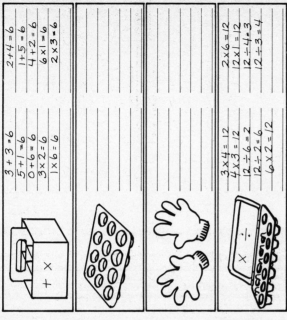

$3 + 3 = 6$ $2 + 4 = 6$
$5 + 1 = 6$ $1 + 5 = 6$
$0 + 6 = 6$ $4 + 2 = 6$
$3 × 2 = 6$ $6 × 1 = 6$
$1 × 6 = 6$ $2 × 3 = 6$

$3 × 4 = 12$ $2 × 6 = 12$
$4 × 3 = 12$ $12 × 1 = 12$
$12 ÷ 6 = 2$ $12 ÷ 4 = 3$
$12 ÷ 2 = 6$ $12 ÷ 3 = 4$
$6 × 2 = 12$ $12 ÷ 2 = 12$

"Basic Math Facts," page 18.
Responses will vary.

SHAPES

Name _____

To the teacher:
Star one or more activities for children to do.

Do the activities that your teacher has starred for you.
Write your answers inside the shapes.
Label each shape.
Measure the area of each shape.
Mark all oblique angles with green, all obtuse angles with red, all right angles with yellow.

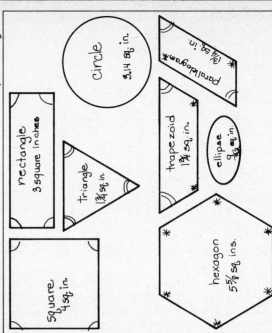

rectangle
3 square inches

Circle
3.14 sq. in.

triangle
1⅛ sq. in.

parallelogram
1¼ sq. in.

square
4 sq. in.

trapezoid
1¾ sq. in.

ellipse
⅞ sq. in.

hexagon
5⅝ sq. ins.

∠ - obtuse
⌐ - right
∟ - oblique

"Geometry," page 19.

COLOR THE SHAPES

Name _____

See how many of these shapes you can find: triangle, square, rectangle, trapezoid, pentagon, parallelogram, hexagon, octagon. It's possible to find at least one of each. Color each type of shape with a different color.

"Geometry," page 21.
Responses will vary.

SHAPE FACE

Name _____

Do one of these activities:
List the kind and number of shapes.
Find the area of each quadrilateral.
Find the area of each enclosed shape.

triangles - 7
rectangles - 11 (including squares)
squares - 6
parallelograms - 1
trapezoids - 1

Option:
Find a picture of a human or animal face.
Redraw the face using geometric shapes for the facial features.

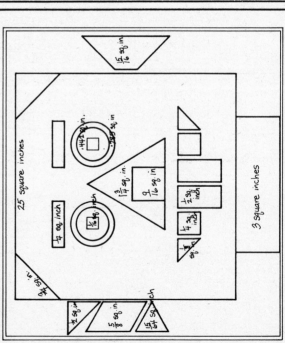

"Geometry," page 24.

THE ITY CITY

Name *Karl*

Write words on the things in the city.

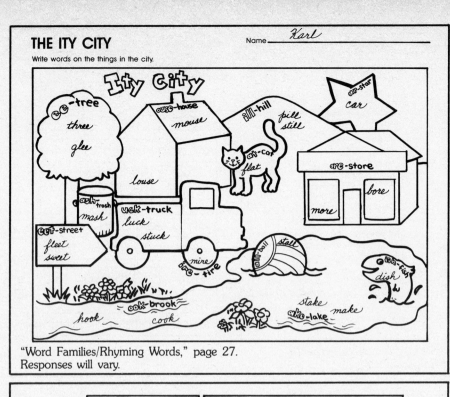

Ity City

tree — three, glee
house — mouse, louse
hill — pill, still
car — star
cat — flat
truck — luck, stuck
trash — mash
street — fleet, sweet
tire — mire
ball — stall
fish — dish
brook — cook, hook
lake — stake, make
store — more, bore

"Word Families/Rhyming Words," page 27.
Responses will vary.

BLANKETY-BLANK-BLANK

Name *Randall*

Complete each poem shown below.
1. Use the WORD LIST boxes to make lists of rhyming words for your poem.
2. Words on the same kind of lines must rhyme.
3. Words on each line must fit the clue written under the line.

POEM #1: NONSENSE
This poem doesn't need to make a lot of sense.

Track , *pack*
any word

rack
any word

How can you *stack* ?
a verb

Change the vowel(s)

to make it *trick*
any word

pick , *stick*
any word   any word

Rick
any word

WORD LISTS for Poem #1
lack   pack
track   rack
sack
stack

trick

POEM #2: PEOPLE POEM

Sammy *Mommy*
person's name person's name

and *Tammy*
person's name

went to the *school*
a place

Ned *Ted*
person's name person's name

and *Fred*
person's name

saw the *pool*
a thing

WORD LISTS For Poem #2
Sammy Tammy
Mommy

Ned
Ted
Fred

school
pool
tool

POEM #3: A LOONY LIMERICK
This poem follows all of the rules, except that the words you write in the boxes do not need to rhyme with each other or with any other word in the poem.

The *rat* *bore* a *large* *coat*

The *cat* asked *"Does* it *float?"*

The *rat* said *"No*

But *it* can *row*

Now *I* need a *boat*

WORD LISTS for Poem #3
cat   flat
hat   rat

coat   boat
float oat

no   tie   low
row   row

"Word Families/Rhyming Words," page 27.
Responses will vary.

VOWELS TEST

Name _____

To the teacher:
Any or all sections may be used, depending on the skills to be evaluated. Responses may be oral and recorded by teacher or aide, or children may write responses according to directions in each section.

A
Say the name of the picture. Write the vowel you hear next to each picture.

B
Say the word. Write the vowel you hear next to each word.

hit — ĭ
hate — ā
foe — ō
use — ū
clap — ă

knee — ē
mop — ŏ
gum — ŭ
ice — ī
bed — ĕ

C
Say the name of each picture. Use different colored crayons or different numbers to show which pictures have the same vowel sound.

D
Read each list of words. Draw a line between each pair of words that have the same vowel sound.

1
shirt
day
ouch
flaw
look
toy
few
toad
thread
ear

2
plow
bought
Bert
soil
could
cute
steer
soul
said
weigh

"Vowels," page 31.

ANATOMY OF A VOWEL

Name *Irene*

Directions:
1. Use this worksheet with your reading book or some other written material.
2. Write in words from your reading that have the same sound and spelling pattern as the words that label each body part.
3. Read the words you listed to a friend.

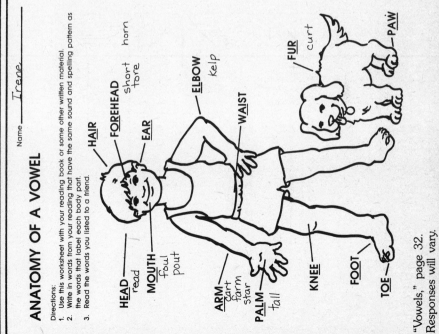

HAIR
FOREHEAD — short, tore
EAR
HEAD — read
MOUTH — foul, pout
ARM — cart, farm, star
PALM — tall
ELBOW — kelp
WAIST
KNEE
FOOT
TOE
horn
FUR — curt
PAW

"Vowels," page 32.
Responses will vary.

NEW ADDITIONS TO THE DICTIONARY

Name: Paul

Follow the directions at the top of each column to complete the worksheet.

Use these marks to show the sounds of the vowels in the words below: long ‾ short ˘ silent ✗	Write a real word that has the same vowel sound	Make up a definition for the "new" word	Use the "new" word in a sentence to show its meaning
pōte	soak	pote- a rip or tear in fabric	I have a pote in my new shirt.
shăx			
chep			
liēg			
dup			
swāp			
bı̄te			
tēap			
cŏm			
flēem			
lŏak			
dı̄nd			

"Vowels," page 32.
Responses will vary.

REARRANGING SENTENCES

Name: Suzanne

The order of the words in our sentences is very important to what we want to say and how we want it to sound.

Play around with the order of each set of words to develop as many sentences that "make sense" as you can.

You can cut out and move words around, if you wish.

You must add punctuation to your finished sentences.

You may form questions.

Use all words in each set in each sentence you make up.

SET 1: Sam a runner is fast
Is Sam a fast runner?
A fast runner is Sam.

SET 2: a dog brown saw a little the cat ball with
A little brown dog saw the cat with a ball.
A brown cat saw a dog with a little ball.

SET 3: silly over boy jumped elephant fat the the
The silly boy jumped over the fat elephant.

SET 4: spaceship meteor the flash with in a a silver collided glowing
In a flash, the silver spaceship collided
with a glowing meteor.

Can you fill the back of this page with at least four more sentences for each set?

"Writing Sentences," page 38.
Responses will vary.

Word tiles:
| Sam | a | runner | is | fast |

a	dog	brown	saw	a
little	the	cat
ball	with

| silly | over | boy | jumped |
| elephant | fat | the | the |

spaceship	meteor	the
flash	with	in	a	a
silver	collided	glowing

SENTENCE FRAGMENTS/PICTURE FRAGMENTS

Name: Georgia

The following sentences and pictures are incomplete. Beginnings, middles, or ends are missing. Fill in the missing parts of the sentences (with words) and pictures (with drawings).

We played and built sand castles **by the sea.**

The strawberry **Soda pop fizzled** and tickled my nose.

The beautiful green snake

red ribbon on the package.

down the street.

through the clouds.

The pilot

"Writing Sentences," page 38.
Responses will vary.

SENTENCE EXPANDER

Name: Kara

Directions:

Read sentence 1 in part A. In the empty boxes write two words to tell what kind of monster.

In sentence 2, the new words you add will tell what kind of boy.

In sentence 3, your new words will tell where the monster was or what the monster was doing.

Expand the sentences in parts B and C, just like you did in part A.

Example:
Expand sentences.
You can expand sentences.
You can expand sentences to make them more interesting.

A

1. The boy saw a | large | scaly (what kind of?) | monster.

2. The | tall | thin (what kind of?) | boy saw a | large | scaly (words from sentence 1) | monster.

3. The | tall | thin (words from sentence 2) | boy saw a | large | scaly (words from sentence 1) | monster | in | the | lagoon (where? or doing what?)

B

1. The sun came up | at | dawn (where or when?)

2. The | huge | orange (what kind of?) | sun came up | at | dawn (words from sentence 1)

3. At | the | beach (when? or where?) | the | huge | orange (words from sentence 2) | sun came up | at | dawn (words from sentence 1)

C

1. People are funny.

2. Silly (what kind of?) | people are | very (how?) | funny.

3. Silly (what kind of?) | people are | very (word from sentence 2) | funny | because they | laugh (why?) | and giggle.

"Writing Sentences," page 39.
Responses will vary.

PUNCTUATION POWER

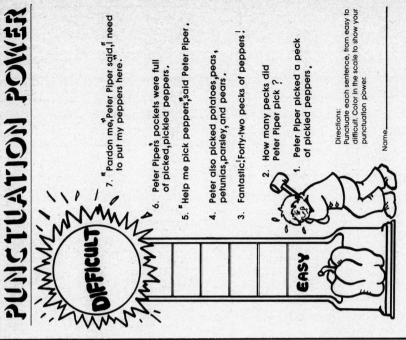

DIFFICULT

7. "Pardon me," Peter Piper said, "I need to put my peppers here."

6. Peter Piper's pockets were full of picked, pickled peppers.

5. "Help me pick peppers," said Peter Piper.

4. Peter also picked potatoes, peas, petunias, parsley, and pears.

3. Fantastic! Forty-two pecks of peppers!

2. How many pecks did Peter Piper pick?

1. Peter Piper picked a peck of pickled peppers.

EASY

Directions:
Punctuate each sentence, from easy to difficult. Color in the scale to show your punctuation power.

Name _____

"Punctuation," page 43.

PUNCTUATION PATTERNS

Name *Glenn*

Fill in the blanks with words to make sentences that use the punctuation marks correctly.

1. I broke home bugs,
   rocks, leaves, and feathers.
2. Hour old are you?
3. "I love to camp."
4. said Sam.
5. No, Not, now, I
   don't have time now.
6. Great game!
7. ...?"
8. ..."?"
9. ..."
10. ...!"

"Punctuation," page 45.
Responses will vary.

BOTHERSOME BUGS

Name *Anne*

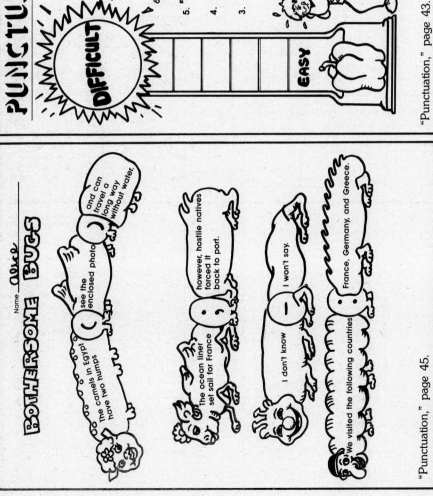

see the enclosed photo and can travel a long way without water. The camels in Egypt have two humps.

however, hostile natives forced it back to port. The ocean liner set sail for France.

I won't say. I don't know.

We visited the following countries: France, Germany, and Greece.

"Punctuation," page 45.

TIME CAPSULE PUNCTUATION

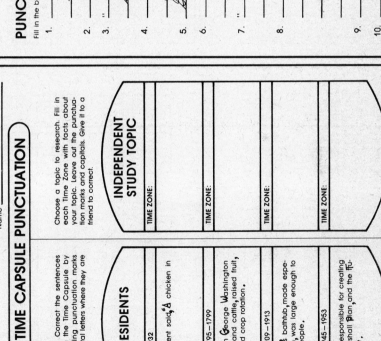

Name _____

Correct the sentences in the Time Capsule by adding punctuation marks and capital letters where they are needed.

PRESIDENTS

TIME ZONE: 1932
Which president said, "A chicken in every pot?"

TIME ZONE: 1795–1799
At Mt. Vernon George Washington bred horses and cattle, raised fruit, and practiced crop rotation.

TIME ZONE: 1909–1913
President Taft's bathtub, made especially for him, was large enough to hold three people.

TIME ZONE: 1945–1953
Truman was responsible for creating NATO, the Marshall Plan, and the Truman Doctrine.

Choose a topic to research. Fill in each Time Zone with facts about your topic. Leave out the punctuation marks and capitals. Give it to a friend to correct.

INDEPENDENT STUDY TOPIC

TIME ZONE: _____

TIME ZONE: _____

TIME ZONE: _____

TIME ZONE: _____

"Punctuation," page 47.

PUNCTUATION P's AND Q's

Name __Louise__

Use the punctuation marks and words to make sentences. Add any other words or punctuation marks you need.

? .	problem popular queer
! .	quit phone poor	Quit it! The poor cracked phone might break!
" "	quiver quake prince	
?	purple quart	Is Mели quart of grape juice purple?
! .	quarantine queen parrot	

Write your initials here. _L.J._
Fill in each box with words that begin with your initials. Use the punctuation marks and words to make sentences. Add any other words or punctuation marks you need.

? " " .	Lion angry Joe	"Is that lion angry?" asked the girl visiting the zoo.
! .		
! ! ?		
! !		

"Punctuation," page 48.
Responses will vary.

USE YOUR NAME

Name __David__

Directions:
1. Spell out your name in the boxes across the top.
2. Under each letter, write parts of speech that begin with that letter. Use adjectives that modify the nouns and adverbs that modify the verbs you've written for each letter.
3. Write a sentence for each group of words in a column. You will need to add other words and punctuation.

	D	A	V	I	D		
NOUN	dragon	artist					
ADJECTIVE	dumb	amateur					
VERB	dance	argue					
ADVERB	divinely	angrily					

The dumb dragon danced divinely.

"Parts of Speech," page 50.
Responses will vary.

PARTS-OF-SPEECH DOMINOES

Name ____

Directions:
1. Cut out the word dominoes.
2. Paste them in the space below in a domino pattern. The sides of the dominoes that touch must be the same part of speech—noun, verb, adjective, or adverb.
3. On the blank half of any domino write a word to make the parts of speech match.

START HERE:

adj.	v. or n.
big	sing

adv.	adv. or n.	adj.
gaily	down	that

n. or v.	n. or v.	n.
tree	sun	man

v. or n.	adj.	adv.
swim	blue	very

"Parts of Speech," page 50.
Responses will vary.

USING THE DICTIONARY

Name ____
Beginning Time ____
Ending Time ____

MY WORK	TEACHER'S COMMENTS

1. Circle the pair of guide words that would be listed on the page where these words are found.

   raccoon — rabbit – razor
   race – reach
   spaghetti – shell – space
   smell – string

2. Look up these words. Write the definition for each.

   judge ____
   suddenly ____
   reimburse ____

3. Divide these words into syllables.

   habitat   hab-i-tat
   peppermint   pep-per-mint
   society   so-ci-e-ty

4. Rewrite each list in alphabetical order.

   fig   berry   deer
   pear   fig   dial
   berry   lemon   dime
   lemon   orange   dog
   orange   pear   dozen
            deer   dial

5. Pronounce these words for the teacher.
   a. kee-hohl   e. pou-der
   b. fayz'   f. pik'-cher
   c. skip'-r   g. mär'-shən
   d. swohp   h. ri-dōōs'

"Using the Dictionary," page 55.

SENSIBLE SYNONYMS

Name _Larry_

Answer the questions using synonyms for the underlined words.

Example:
Would you feign sickness?
No, I would not pretend to be sick.

1. Would you gawk at an elephant in a tree?
   I would stare at an elephant in a tree.

2. Would eating a gallon of ice cream make you feel ecstatic?
   I'd be very, very happy eating so much ice cream.

3. How would you look if you were morose?
   I would have a sad face if I were morose.

4. Are you in the mood for a succulent food?

5. What is the last thing you imbibed today?

6. Would a humdrum movie interest you?

7. Would you pull the hair of a languid bear?

8. Is a potpourri something to cook in?

9. Would you rather criticize an ostrich or ostracize a critic?

10. Why does the hound make that guttural sound?

"Using the Dictionary," page 56.
Responses will vary.

DESIGN A DICTIONARY PAGE

Name _Samantha_

Directions:
1. Select nine words for your dictionary page.
2. Complete the worksheet by including all the parts used in a dictionary page, such as guide word, entry word, pronunciation, definition, illustration (for one of the words), and part of speech.

apple _____ rod

apple (ap'-l) n. a
red, yellow, or green
fruit

(   )   (   )

(   )   (   )

rabbit (rab'-it, n. a
fast
animal

(   )   rod (rŏd) n
                a long, straight pole

"Using the Dictionary," page 57.
Responses will vary.

WORDS, WORDS, WORDS

Each time your shape appears you must fill it in with the information asked for. Some words you might like to use: novel, drone, produce, inducement.

TEAM MEMBERS: ○ – George □ – Howard △ – Lynne

WORD	novel	inducement	
GUIDE WORDS	note mow	indigo inductive	
SYLLABLES	nov-l	in-duce-ment	
ONE DEFINITION	new, unusual	act of influencing or persuading	

"Using the Dictionary," page 57.
Responses will vary.

PREFIX AND SUFFIX SERVICE, INC.

Directions:
Fill in the top of the worksheet. Use the information in the PART(S) and QUANTITY columns to make words. Write the words in the LABOR column. Note any spelling changes in the SERVICE column.

Name _____
Address _____   Date _____
City _____ State _____ Zip Code _____
Telephone _____

PART(S)	QUANTITY	LABOR	SERVICE
ANCE	2 words	reliance repentance	change y to i
RE	3 words	return review resale	
TION	6 words		
UN	4 words		
DIS, LY	5 words		
FUL	2 words		
SUB	3 words		
LESS	5 words		
ENT	2 words		

"Prefixes and Suffixes," page 62.
Responses will vary.

AT YOUR SERVICE

Name _Mark_

Directions:
1. Write the name of a job or business you would like to have – for example, TV repair-person. _T.V. Repairman_
2. On the shapes below, write slogans or ads related to the job you chose, using as many words as you can that have prefixes and suffixes.
3. Underline or circle each prefix or suffix you use.

(Reliable and dependable) service
Mark's T.V.
Phone 222-2202
Economical Rentals

Mark's T.V. Service
(Unconditional) warranty available

MARKS T.V.
Repair & Rental

Color Specialists
Factory authorization
phone: 222-2202

Mark's T.V.

Fill in your business card, including a slogan and a short description of your business or service.

Write a slogan for your workclothes.

Write a slogan on your badge.

Write a slogan or ad on your truck.

"Prefixes and Suffixes," page 63.
Responses will vary.

PREFIX/SUFFIX CROSSWORD

Name _____

Directions:
Complete this puzzle in the usual way. Some new things you will need to know to complete it are:
1. Boxes for all pre-fixes and suf-fixes are out-lined in darker lines.
2. In the clues, the capital words tell you the meanings of the prefixes and suf-fixes that you will use.
3. All root words needed in the puzzle can be found in some form in the clue.

Crossword answers: DISLOCATE, INTENSIFY, RELATIONSHIP, GRADUATION, ENSNARE, UNEASY, UNSPEAKABLE, APTLESSLY, SUBWAY

ACROSS
2. to TAKE AWAY or MOVE FROM the usual location
3. THE STATE OF being related
5. NOT at ease
8. NOT POSSIBLE to speak of
11. ACT OF being graduated
13. to catch IN a trap or snare

DOWN
1. TO MAKE more intense
4. ABLE to be resisted
6. STATE OF BEING NOT happy
7. IN A MANNER INDICATING LACK Of tact
9. design AGAIN
9. FILLED WITH beauty
10. MANNER of being neat

"Prefixes and Suffixes," page 63.

PREFIX/SUFFIX TIC-TAC-TOE

Names _____ (player 1)
_____ (player 2)
(2 players)

Directions:
In each game, decide who will be P and who will be S (flip a coin or draw). P marks prefixes; S marks suffixes. The youngest player begins the game.
1. Choose a square and find the word that contains your word part.
2. Read the word and spell the prefix or suffix.
3. If you are correct, the square is yours and you may mark it. If you are wrong, the square belongs to the other player.
4. Settle any disagreements with a dictionary.

Game 1 Winner _____
Game 2 Winner _____ Game 3 Winner _____

GAME 1

sleepless understand uncover	helpful story unaware	outside rearrange partnership
displace exclamation butcher	rechargeable sidewalk unleash	forgetful discontent lumber
enjoyment repair parade	proclaim difference restaurant	snowman painless subhuman

GAME 2

coexist comfort disappearance	happiness rename purple	plastic decode fulfillment
cooperate painful product	distaste favorable recognize	reletter cupful relation
beside homeward direction	attempt homeless disbelief	return backward jingle

GAME 3

portion afterward preoccupy	restate fearless toothpaste	action inside retell
parlor kindness preview	bemoan armchair lamentable	playful liquid regain
playground undecidedly rejoin	promotion cowboy antifreeze	seasonal sportsmanship interact

"Prefixes and Suffixes," page 63.
Responses will vary.

MAIN IDEA

Name _____

Teri

II. ✓ the number that matches the topic sentence.
___ 1 ___ 2 ___ 3 ✓ 4
1. The rose is a flower that is often used for corsages. 2 The chrysanthemum is a flower that is eaten. 3 Some flowers are used to make teas. 4 Flowers are used for a variety of purposes.

I. Fill in the bubble that names the letter of the topic sentence.
Ⓐ Ⓑ Ⓒ Ⓓ Ⓔ
● ○ ○ ○ ○
A There are many different kinds and locations of homes. B Some homes are small. C Some homes are big. D Some homes are near the city. E Where do you live?

IV. Write or tell your teacher the main idea of the picture in your own words.
There are many things to see and do at the circus.

III. Write the letter that names the topic sentence. _C_
ᴬCinderella was crying. ᴮHer stepsis-ters were angry. ᶜEveryone in the house was upset. ᴰThe cat was running around. ᴱThe dog was barking.

VI. List the key words of the paragraph below.
names, fish
shape, color
yellow-tail, tuna
pink salmon
Names of fish often give clues to their many different shapes and col-ors. There are yellow-tail tunas and pink salmon. Can you guess the shapes of the pipefish and the ham-merhead shark?

V. Write the main idea of the story in your own words. _Mary and_ _her dog did many things together._
Mary had a dog as a pet. They played together. They watched TV together. They went everywhere to-gether.

To the teacher:
Check the appropriate column to indi-cate the student's performance on these main-idea exercises.

ITEM	RESPONDED APPROPRIATELY	NEEDS PRACTICE
Locates topic sentence in context (I, II, III)		
States main idea from picture or paragraph (IV, V)		
Identifies key words (VI)		

"Main Idea/Summarizing," page 67.

MAIN STREET

Name _____ *Rick*

Directions:
For each Main Street, read a paragraph, chapter, or story. Write a key word from what you have read in each building. Use the key words to write a main-idea statement on Main Street.

Story Source: *The Moffats By Eleanor Estes*

Miss Myles | *calling* | *Joey* | *Jane* | *shy* | *red automobile*

Main Street *Jane and Joey Moffat go calling on Miss Myles, their teacher. Joey wants to tell Miss Myles about the red automobile, but is unable to talk because he is so shy.*

Story Source: _____

Main Street _____

Story Source: _____

Main Street _____

"Main Idea/Summarizing," page 68.
Responses will vary.

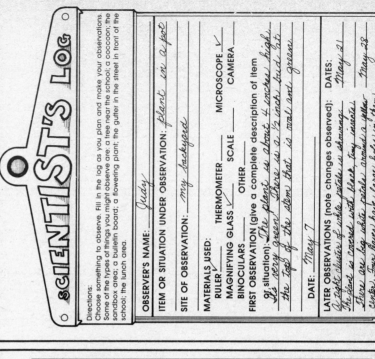

SCIENTIST'S LOG

Directions:
Choose something to observe. Fill in the log as you plan and make your observations. Some of the types of things you might observe are: a tree near the school; a cocoon; the sandbox area; a bulletin board; a flowering plant; the gutter in the street in front of the school; the lunch area.

OBSERVER'S NAME: _____ *Judy*

ITEM OR SITUATION UNDER OBSERVATION: *plant in a pot*

SITE OF OBSERVATION: *my backyard*

MATERIALS USED:
RULER ✓   THERMOMETER ____   MICROSCOPE ✓
MAGNIFYING GLASS ✓   SCALE ____   CAMERA ____
BINOCULARS ____   OTHER ____

FIRST OBSERVATION (give a complete description of item or situation): *The plant is about 4 inches high. Its very green. There is a ½ inch bud at the top of the stem that is oval and green.*

DATE: *May 7*

LATER OBSERVATIONS (note changes observed):   DATES:
A tight cluster of white petals is showing.   *May 21*
The plant is covered with black, tiny insects.
There are big white petals around a yellow   *May 28*
center. Four leaves have grown below in them.

"Observation," page 74.
Responses will vary.

SENSES TAKING

Name *LaVerne*

A trip to *the zoo*

In the first column, name the stops you make on your trip. In the other columns, describe what you see, hear, smell, taste, and feel at each stop.

STOPS YOU MAKE	👁	👂	👃	👄	✋
food stand	popcorn popping	popcorn crackling	buttery smell	salty taste	bumpy feeling
reptile house	dark and shady	people whispering	smells musty	✗	glass on cages feels clammy

"Observation," page 78.
Responses will vary.

SEEING RELATIONSHIPS

Name *Benjamin*

CATEGORIZING:
Put an X on the pictures that belong in the same group as a ball. These belong in the same group because they are used in games with a ball.

bat | net | Pin-ball machine | button | donut | wheel | croquet stick | tennis racket

CATEGORIZING:
Add three more pictures that belong in the group. These belong in the group because

CAUSE AND EFFECT: Match each cause to its effect by drawing connecting lines.

CAUSES
He put too much air in the ball.
The batter hit a home run.
The golfer hit the ball into a window.

EFFECTS
The ball went into the stands.
He paid the man $50.00.
He had to buy a new ball.

SEQUENCE: Arrange the pictures in order by putting a number inside each picture.

BRUINS 2 TROJANS 0

3 | — | 4 | 2

OTHER RELATIONSHIPS: Teacher-designed activity to assess student's ability to understand other relationships such as time, place, and analogies.

"Seeing Relationships," page 79.

CLASSIFYING

Cut out the numbered squares. Lay out all the squares that go under column A and write the numbers under the column heading. Return these squares to the others. Now find all the squares for column B and write their numbers. Continue until you have completed all the columns.

1. ball
2.
3.
4.
5.
6. board
7.
8. hockey puck
9.
10.
11. mitt
12. cookie
13. cow
14. dime
15.
16.
17.
18.
19.
20. pie
21.
22.
23.
24.

Name _____

H things you wear on your hands	8, 11, 21
G sharp metal things	3, 16, 18, 19
F growing things	22, 24
E rubber sports items	4, 13, 15, 23
D one-syllable words	1, 8, 23
C wooden things	1, 3, 4, 6, 7, 10, 18, 14, 18, 20, 21, 22
B sports things	2, 4, 6
A round man-made things	1, 5, 8, 10, 10, 17, 1, 5, 8, 12, 11, 17, 23, 14, 20, 21

"Seeing Relationships," page 80.   Responses will vary.

CAUSE-AND-EFFECT BINGO

Name _____

To use as a worksheet for one person:
1. Find an effect to match each cause.
2. Indicate matching causes and effects with the same number. Use a new number for each pair you find.

	1	2	3	4	5
C	When the roller coaster sped down the steepest incline. 6	flood 10	15	16	earthquake 20
A	When he shook the pop bottle before opening. 11	17	Because he found his lost dog. 21
U	John carried the ball into the end zone. 12	13	springtime 18	FREE 22	tic-tac-toe 23
S	FREE	missed catching a fly ball	1			
E	He didn't feed his goldfish 5	so they died.	a flat tire 7	birds building nests, flowers blooming 18
E	16	smog	1		everyone screamed. 6
F	The team scored six points. 12		17	the soda squirted out. 11
F	FREE	he was happy.	FREE	
E	The boy was dressed as Dracula 22	21	8	homeless people 15
C	The winner 3	thunder 9			
T	4			error in baseball 14

"Seeing Relationships," page 81.
Note: Some causes may be matched to more than one effect; for example, causes A-1 and S-3 could be matched to either smog or the picture of people coughing.

DRAWING CONCLUSIONS

	ASSIGNMENTS (for teacher use)

Check the evidence that supports the conclusion.

CONCLUSION
The pet got out of the cage.

EVIDENCE
✓ the cage was empty.
__ The pet was hiding under the newspaper in the cage.
✓ Nobody could find the pet.
✓ Everyone saw the pet run away.

Write a conclusion for the evidence.

CONCLUSION
People went to a party (responses will vary)

EVIDENCE
People were happy.
Cake was served.
Presents were opened.
Everyone sang.

Match each conclusion with evidence.

CONCLUSION
Mickey Mouse is Donald Duck's friend.

Mickey Mouse is famous.

Mickey Mouse is a cartoon character.

EVIDENCE
His picture is in the Hall of Fame and watches have his picture on them.

He is drawn by someone and doesn't really talk.

He is shown holding hands with him and they play together.

"Drawing Conclusions," page 85.

CHARACTER CONCLUSIONS

Name _Kim_

Author _Spyri_

Story Title _Heidi_

Directions:
1. Write the names of three characters from a story you've read.
2. Write in a feeling you think each character had at some time during the story.
3. List evidence from the story that seems to prove the character felt this way.

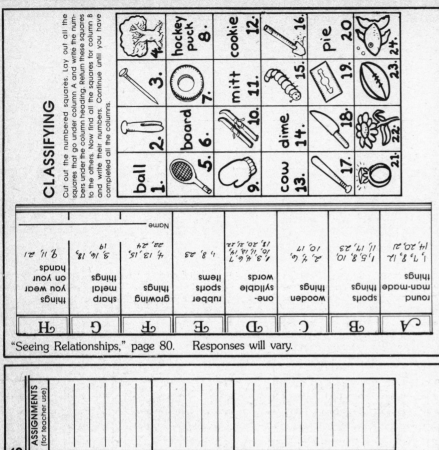

CHARACTER'S NAME
Heidi

FEELING
lonely

EVIDENCE
She talked about her grandfather and wanted to visit him.

CHARACTER'S NAME

FEELING

EVIDENCE

CHARACTER'S NAME

FEELING

EVIDENCE

"Drawing Conclusions," page 86.
Responses will vary.

HOPPING TO CONCLUSIONS

Name _____

Directions:
1. Read a conclusion on the lily pad.
2. Read the list of evidence.
3. Mark the numbers on the jumping path that match the pieces of evidence needed to reach the conclusion.
4. Draw the jumping pattern the frog will use to get to the lily pad by connecting the numbers like this:

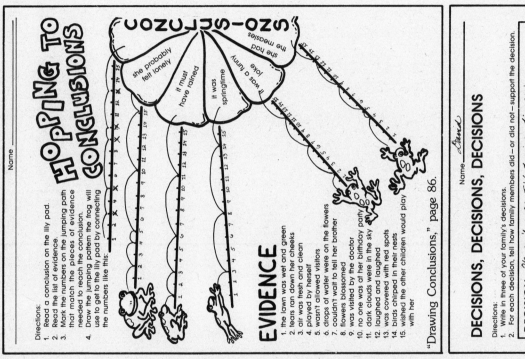

Lily pad conclusions: CONCLUSIONS — she probably felt lonely — It must have rained — it was springtime — It was a funny joke — she had the measles

EVIDENCE
1. the lawn was wet and green
2. tears ran down her cheeks
3. air was fresh and clean
4. played by herself
5. wasn't allowed visitors
6. drops of water were on the flowers
7. couldn't wait to tell her brother
8. flowers blossomed
9. was visited by the doctor
10. no one was at her birthday party
11. dark clouds were in the sky
12. laughed and laughed
13. was covered with red spots
14. birds chirped in their nests
15. wished the other children would play with her

"Drawing Conclusions," page 86.

DECISIONS, DECISIONS, DECISIONS

Name _Sarah_

Directions:
1. Write in three of your family's decisions.
2. For each decision, tell how family members did—or did not—support the decision.

DECISION *We can't watch T.V. during dinner.*

Family Member	Supporting/Not Supporting the Decision
Mom	It's bad for your digestion.
Bobby	We'd argue over what to watch.
Me	I'd rather talk.
Dad	nothing to say

DECISION *Everyone should help with the garden.*

Family Member	Supporting/Not Supporting the Decision

DECISION *Each person gets to plan and make/specify meal each week.*

Family Member	Supporting/Not Supporting the Decision

"Drawing Conclusions," page 90.
Responses will vary.

INDEX